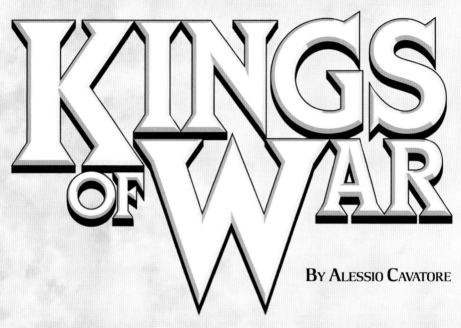

KINGS OF WAR

By Alessio Cavatore

FOREWORD

When asked to write these few introductory words I hardly expected to find myself writing the foreword to what is undoubtedly now the most popular mass-battle fantasy game on the market! What I was expecting was to be able to say that Kings of War has come of age with this, its second edition, always something of a milestone in the history of a game. I would have – and can still – acknowledge that the original Kings of War game has gained a loyal and growing following amongst fantasy wargamers. Many converts have found themselves won over by a mixture of solid game play, straight-forward but elegant mechanics, and an approach to development that plainly puts the player first. This new edition represents another stride in the same direction, and is sure to appeal both to existing devotees and to those discovering the game for the first time.

So well done Mantic – and well done especially to its creator and designer Alessio Cavatore. I have worked together with Alessio on many gaming projects over the years, both historical and fantasy, and have always appreciated his clear and focussed approach to game design, instinct for uncluttered rules, and – most of all – boundless and unquenchable enthusiasm for games and gaming. I think I can confidently say that you'll find plenty of those qualities in Kings of War along with the surety and experience that always comes with a second edition. So, enough from me, muster the ranks for battle and ready the beasts, let arrows fly and dice roll, for now is the time for Kings of War.

Rick Priestley

INTRODUCTION

Welcome to Kings of War!

Kings of War is a mass-battle fantasy wargame set in the world of Mantica, taking all of the fantasy archetypes and embedding them into a rich history full of exciting characters and enigmatic new races. This book contains all of the core rules for the game, along with complete army lists for eleven different forces, and a selection of magical artefacts for them to carry into battle.

This latest edition brings together everything that we've learnt in the last six years, after a very popular first edition, two Kickstarters, an ever-growing miniatures range, and thousands of games. The loyal fans who have been with us through the previous editions will be able to see the progress that has been made. We simply couldn't have done this without our wonderful community – the copious amounts of feedback and many long hours of hard work from our volunteer Rules Committee have made this the most solid set of rules we've ever put out – we couldn't be prouder. Huge thanks to every one of you.

The game itself is very fast to play and easy to learn, but it will take time and experience to master. With few and simple rules, there is little to get in the way of the fun and carnage of epic tabletop battles where huge armies clash. Mantic's affordable prices enable you to build an affordable and great-looking army that's simple to assemble and paint. This unobtrusive rule set makes Kings of War a challenging game of strategy, much like chess. Kings of War allows you to pit your wits against your opponent, the battlefield and the strengths and weaknesses of your own army... and, of course, the dice! The innovative turn structure lets you play Kings of War using a stopwatch or a chess clock. As the seconds tick away, the pressure and excitement makes Kings of War unlike any other large-scale war game you've ever played before.

On our website, you'll find free introductory rules and army lists so that you can introduce your friends and club members to the new and exciting world of the Kings of War game. On our forums, you can leave your opinions, ideas and feedback. Please keep it coming!

www.manticgames.com/Forum.html

Devastation and slaughter await...

CONTENTS

A WORLD AT WAR 4

A History of Mantica 6

Mantica............. 18

THE RULES 46

Units 48

The Turn 52

Move 54

Terrain 58

Shoot............... 60

Melee 64

Nerve............... 68

War Engines 70

Individuals 71

Special Rules 72

Picking a Force 76

Magical Artefacts 78

Spells 82

Game Scenarios 84

Timed Games 88

FORCE LISTS 90

Forces of Basilea 92

Dwarf Armies 104

Elf Armies.......... 118

Kingdoms of Men 130

Forces of Nature...... 138

Ogre Armies 148

Forces of the Abyss ... 156

Abyssal Dwarfs....... 166

Goblin Armies 176

Orc Armies 186

Undead Armies....... 194

Modelling Units 206

CREDITS

Game Design
Alessio Cavatore

Kings of War Rules Committee
Matt Gilbert, Daniel King, Sami Mahmoud,
Chris Morris, Mark Smith, Nick Williams

Background
Michael Grey, Guy Haley, Mark Latham,
Thomas Pike, Anthony Reynolds, Greg D Smith

Sculpting
Gregor Adrian, Juan Miguel López Barea,
Ben Calvert-Lee, Russ Charles, Gregory
Clavilier, Derek Miller, Gary Morley, Bob
Naismith, Dave Neild, Nicolas Nguyen, Juan
Navarro Perez, Tim Prow, Sylvain Quirion,
Steve Saunders, Ben Skinner, Luigi Terzi,
Remy Tremblay, James van Schaik, Kevin White

Painting
Luke Barker, Mark Bedwell, Andrew Chesney,
Conflict in Colour, Matt Gilbert, Golem
Painting Studio, Dave Neild, Paul Scott
Miniatures, Chris Straw, Chris Webb, Andrew
Wedmore, Nick Williams, Winterdyne
Commission Modelling

Art
Robin Carey, Shen Fei, Roberto Cirillo,
Heath Foley, Des Hanley, Yann Hoarau,
Ralph Horsley, Stef Kopinski, Alan Lathwell,
Phil Moss, Michael Rechlin, Jonas Springborg,
Luigi Terzi

Graphic Design
Pete Borlace, Kev Brett, Karen Miksza,
Dylan Owen, Sean Turtle, Chris Webb

Photography
Warwick Kinrade, Mike McVey, Ben Sandum,
Adam Shaw

Playtesters
Sam Rounsevell, Jason Flint, Jason Moorman,
Jez Gurney, Chris "Baz" Beeson, John Beeson,
N. Carpenter, Adam Storey, Bartjan van Kolck,
Asbjørn-Heike Hagen, Andrew Massoura,
HeroicTheNerd

Special Thanks
Warlord Games, Fireforge Games, Gripping
Beast, Artisan Designs and Conquest
Miniatures.

All scenery from owner's collection.

Mantic Games, 193 Hempshill Lane, Bulwell, Nottingham, NG6 8PF, UK

www.manticgames.com

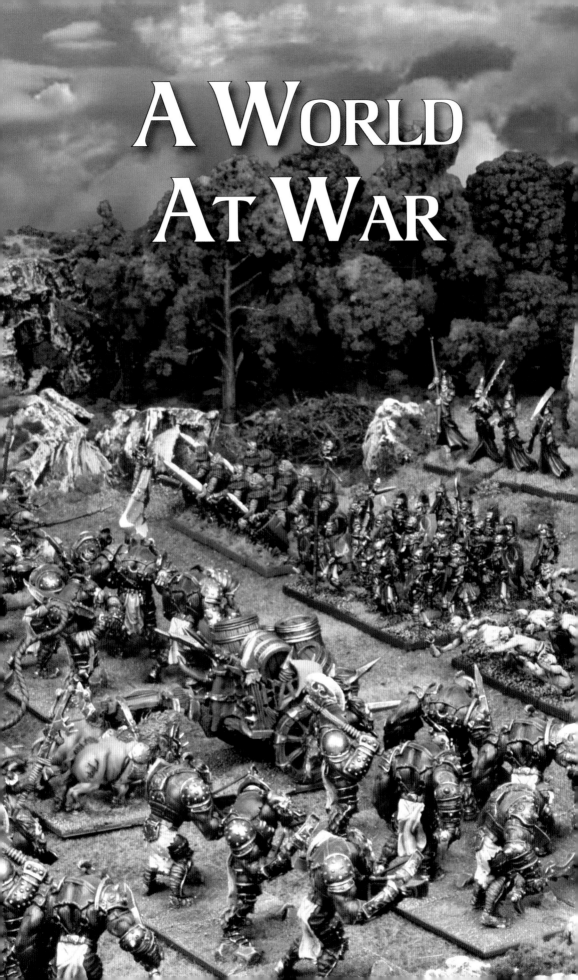

A WORLD AT WAR

A HISTORY OF MANTICA

Once, the world was in balance. That time is no more; it is an age recorded only in dusty scrolls or on the monuments of drowned cities. It is little more than a legend, for those who live in Mantica today remember little but war. There are, perhaps, some who remember better days – those half-gods or near-immortals gifted in sorcery – but if so, they hold their silence.

Since ancient times, the world has been ravaged by war. The wise foresee an age of horror approaching, for the spirit of the earth is sick, tainted by deadly sorcery in a great conflict ages past. Not that the warlords of this bloody era care, not while there is glory to be won, territory to be wrested from the enemy, foes to be slaughtered. The so-called Noble Peoples – Men, Elves and Dwarfs – now struggle

for power and influence, battling across the ruins of long-dead realms, or staking claim to new lands. Their ancient pacts are no more. The kingdoms that pledged their armies in service of those sacred treaties are gone into legend, the descendants of the noble princes who swore eternal oaths of friendship warring openly with one another. The glorious empires of those days are lost to the ocean, or buried beneath shifting sands, the palaces of the wise now home to kraken or shambling revenants, while the scions of their great houses are exiled or long-dead.

Men, ever the most adaptable of the Noble Peoples, have taken to this age of conquest with relish. No wilderness, no barren waste, and no monstrous foe can deter these bold peoples from carving their own fledgling

states. Pauper-princes, exiled nobles and upstart knights snatch territory from their rivals by the sword, while common folk are pressed into service daily to defend their lands and their lives. Orcs, Goblins and worse roam the dark places, the high peaks, forbidding forests and frozen plains, a threat to shake the mountains, should they ever unite.

Overall, great danger hangs like storm clouds. As the petty kingdoms of Men vie for dominance, as the relentless Dwarfs extend their boundless under-kingdom, as the Elves sink into despairing dreams of their past glories, the dark mage Mhorgoth stalks the land. The most powerful necromancer ever to have tainted the earth with his existence, vast legions of unliving warriors follow his rotting banners.

To the far north, the evil Abyssal Dwarfs create machines, a fusion of dark sorcery and technology, ready to enslave the world. Within the deep pit of the Abyss, dark gods stir, yearning to break free from their prison and tread the clean earth once again. Their demonic servants are legion, ready to do the bidding of any willing to pay the terrible price of the Abyssals in blood and souls.

There are but a few places where the light of the old era persists, where the remaining deities of noble intent might still be implored for aid, but ranged against such evil, what hope is there for the world? Legions of darkness, stirred to a frenzy by the Wicked Ones, march savagely upon the myriad kingdoms of Men, the scattered

Elven Kindreds and the subterranean holds of the Dwarfs. Mercenaries and adventurers find fame and fortune in battle, while the servants of the Shining Ones cling to a way of life that seems almost lost. Nine hundred years after the last dark god was cast down into the Abyss, Mantica trembles once more to the marching of vast armies.

Serried ranks draw battlelines each day; war horns clamour across fields of glory; ragged banners are held aloft in defiance. Magic flares, monsters roar, the dead rise from shallow graves. The only constant in a world of turmoil is that devastation and slaughter await...

THE TIME OF LIGHT

Things were not always thus. In ancient times three civilisations, whose achievements tower over those of today's benighted world, coexisted in great harmony, bringing much good to all. The Kingdom of the Elves, the Underlands of the Dwarfs, and the Grand Republic of Primovantor – largest realm of Men – ruled a world untroubled by dark magic or the likes of Orcs and Abyssals.

Millennia ago, at the height of these realms' power, all three Noble Peoples worshipped a race of gods known as the Celestians, the Children of the Stars. Their gifts to Man, Dwarf and Elf were mighty, fitting to the talents and hearts of each. Under the guidance of the Celestians, great cities became places of wonder and peace, shining towers reaching to the stars. Beyond the city walls, emerald forests stretched for leagues around, and the creatures of the wild lived in harmony with the three great races. Men walked upon the soil of other planes of existence, the Elves created works of art never surpassed, and the Dwarfs delved their greatest underground cities.

Whence the Celestians came, and whether they were truly gods or some other kind of being, is no longer known. What is recorded, in scraps and fragments, in mildewed tomes in wizards' libraries, and in worn hieroglyphs on the walls of forgotten temples, is how they fell.

CALISOR AND ELINATHORA

Legend tells of the Elven mage Calisor Fenulian, the greatest wizard in all history, whose mastery of arcane lore would not be matched until the coming of Valandor the Great himself, if even then. Where and when he was born is unrecorded, but his entrance to life at the Elven High King's Court is well-known, and his deeds there are half-remembered in innumerable legends and songs. Calisor was said to be so powerful that he could draw the ocean up from its bed, or call the clouds down from the sky. He could step between one plane and the next as easily as a man might walk from one room to another, or even visit other worlds. He was the first to learn the magical speech of the dragons, forging strong bonds between the Elf and Draconic races.

The list of Calisor's feats, when taken together, seems impossible in these times, mere legends – that he could breathe water; that he once jumped to the moon to win a wager; that he could summon pillars of flame and transform them into flocks of birds; that he could know the mind of any whom he touched. An accomplished artist, statesman, and warrior – for although peace was the norm then, war was not unknown – Calisor was the hero of ages.

As is often the way of those who have everything, it was not enough for Calisor.

Perhaps he would have lived his long life out in peace and prosperity had he never have met Elinathora of Primovantor, but it was not to be. Elinathora was the daughter of Marcon, a former Tribune of Esk, one of Primovantor's great cities. Now an elder statesman, much-loved by his people, Marcon was granted a role as an envoy to the Elven city of Therennia Adar, at the time the home of the High King's Court. It was here that Elinathora was first seen by Calisor.

Calisor fell instantly in love with Elinathora, and immediately began to court her. Unions between Man and Elf were not unknown in those times, and many of the great romances of this age refer to the doomed love affairs between short-lived humans and the long-lived Elves. Calisor and Elinathora's is not one of them. She did not reciprocate his affection. The thought of wedding herself to so great an Elf, and living in his shadow forever, and then to die long before he, filled her with something close to terror. Though she was ever polite, and felt a certain friendship for Calisor, she remained firm. She returned his outlandish gifts, and declined to meet with him in private. Initially Calisor was not to be daunted, but over time even his spirit was crushed. His laugh was heard less frequently, and his duties were performed with listlessness, if at all.

Others came to Elinathora on Calisor's behalf, asking that she reconsider, but she

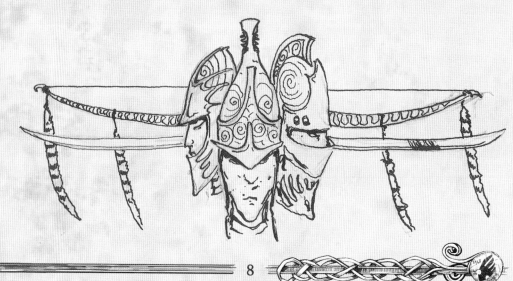

remained true to her decision. Eventually, Calisor left the city, and took to wandering the sacred glades beyond.

Therennia Adar stands to this day, but the vast forests that once surrounded it are drowned beneath the sea. The Sacred Glades the Elves have now are a pale shadow of the original Groves of Adar. Here was great power, for the Celestians themselves were wont to wander beneath the ancient boughs when evening fell.

While Calisor roamed, he chanced upon Oskan, one of the younger Celestians, who stood basking in starlight. Calisor was long accustomed to treating with these god-beings, having gleaned much of their ways in his youth, and the two spoke at length. Oskan could read the hearts of all, and he pressed the warrior-mage to tell him his troubles.

Oskan bade Calisor be calm, and offered to help. He gave Calisor instructions as to the construction of a magical mirror that would show past and future both. If Calisor could make this artefact, the Celestian said, and contrive to have Elinathora gaze into it, she would return his love just as surely as the moon pulls the tides.

And yet Oskan gave Calisor a warning: "There will come a moment during the visions when a golden bird will sing," the Celestian said. "Do not allow her to see beyond this point, and all will be well." Calisor nodded eagerly. For the first time in months his mood lifted. So quick was he in hurrying off to begin the mirror's fabrication that he forgot even to thank Oskan.

The making of the Fenulian Mirror was long and arduous, some say Calisor's greatest task, and the labour of creating such an artefact gave him renewed vigour and purpose. He was obliged to bring together many items of great rarity, including the glimmer of the Star of Heaven, the sacred star that gave the Celestians their power.

The taking of this single ray of light was to have profound consequences.

The Fenulian Mirror

The Elves were pleased to have Calisor some way back to his old self, and they did not query his constant questing. In time, he had all he needed, and he commenced construction of the mirror. It is said the sky split with terrible thunders the day he silvered the glass, and that the sea flooded inland many leagues when he set it in its frame. It was as if the cosmos sought to warn the mage against trifling with such forces. He paid it no attention.

Finally, he was finished. If creating the mirror was a task worthy of a god, it was nothing compared to actually getting Elinathora to look into it. Somehow, he did. Where wit, charm and gifts failed, he pestered her until she acquiesced. And when she did, what things she saw! She saw her future side by side with Calisor Fenulian, a life full of adventure and love. She saw many fine deeds and finer children, she saw a husband devoted to her like no man could be. She saw her life lengthened by her proximity to him, and when old age finally did come upon her, it was a glorious, golden twilight, lived out in a splendid castle with a garden of breathtaking complexity, where she was loved and adored by Men, Dwarves and Elves.

Elinathora's heart began to thaw toward the elf hero, and she cast a sidelong glance at him, and gave a smile such that he near perished with happiness.

In that moment, a sound went unheeded; the sound of birdsong signalling dusk's embrace. Calisor was lost. Too late, he saw the golden bird, singing on a branch in the impossible garden framed by the mirror. His attempts to bring the woman away only made her more intent on watching, and she did not like what she saw.

She saw her own demise, and her corpse rotting in a marble tomb as Calisor grieved outside. She watched as Calisor took lover after lover, trying to drown out her memory and going near mad in the process. She saw the dual natures of her children at war inside them. She saw how one of their

sons grew bitter, and raised an army. She saw him fight his father, and saw him slain.

She saw Calisor die in shame at what he had wrought. Elinathora stepped back from the mirror, shaking her head. "This cannot be, this cannot be," she said. Calisor, distraught, tried to assuage her fears, to no avail. Elinathora, terrified of what might come to pass, smashed the mirror.

THE GOD WAR

The mirror was possessed of the Celestians' essence, and when it was broken, so too were they.

Those Celestians that did not perish were split in twain. Two aspects were birthed by every one, separate entities born of a god, and yet both limited, vengeful, and petty; both lesser than the Celestian they had once been. Each was replaced by a 'Shining' – a good aspect, with a strict and uncompromising morality – and a 'Wicked' aspect, an evil side, an anti-pantheon that relishes destruction and bends its godly talents to all manner of perversity and cruelty. These aspects, though once part of a greater whole, were antithetical to one another, and immediately strife followed as they set upon one another. War followed the split, then war upon war upon war. Countless cities were toppled as the ground heaved at the birth of new gods, and the skies darkened with great storms. Flaming comets fell from the stars; seas boiled; magic ran wild.

Members of all the Noble races were tempted to the evil side, and brother fought brother as madness gripped the world. Many half-gods of both sides were slain, and many powerful magical artefacts used in those ancient conflicts litter some of those forgotten places to this day, the greatest and most pernicious of these abodes being the Abyss, home of all that is evil.

Many among the wise believe that Oskan manipulated Calisor to create the mirror, knowing it would be destroyed, setting in chain a series of events that he, under Celestian law, could not begin. It is suspected that he coveted power, or that he sought revenge for some slight by his fellow deities. Some maintain that Oskan had tired of immortality, and wanted to feel the same passion coursing through his veins that the mortal races felt. Others still maintain that Oskan was unlike the other Celestians – that his dark nature had always lurked beneath the surface, waiting for an opportunity to break loose. In any case, his better half was swiftly trapped and destroyed, and the evil aspect, still calling itself Oskan, became the most bloodthirsty and deadly of all the strange new gods – called by his foes the Father of Lies.

Countless thousands were slain as the God Wars raged for centuries. Kingdoms fell and were laid waste, and with them much knowledge was lost. The evil gods, known as The Wicked Ones, created many foul beings to do their bidding – the ranks of these beasts swelled, and monstrous legions marched upon the lands of Men, Elves and Dwarfs. Only when Domivar the Unyielding, the son of Mescator, God of Justice, and the human woman Laria, High Consul of Primovantor, fought with Oskan were the wars brought to a close. As armies a hundred thousand strong fought upon the ground, Domivar embraced his destiny and took the divine form of his father, soaring into the sky on powerful wings.

There, amid sorcerous lightning and roiling black cloud he clashed with Oskan, Father of Lies. Oskan had become mighty indeed, feeding upon all the evil he had unleashed

upon the world, and his form had become monstrous and incredibly strong. Nevertheless, Domivar bested him that day, taking from Oskan's grasp his deadly Black Axe, a terrible thing said to have been forged of the cold, endless black between the stars. Domivar struck the ground with it, tearing a great rent in the earth. Into this Abyss he cast the majority of the evil gods, imprisoning them there.

With this mighty task complete, so too was Domivar's divine power spent. With the essence of his Celestian father leaving him, Domivar returned to his mortal form and fell from the sky. His body was found, broken and scarred, on the edge of the precipice, next to the hellish pit he had created.

THE TIME OF ICE

For thousands of years, a semblance of what went before returned, although far lesser in degree, for much had been lost, and Mantica was now home to many wicked things that before had not existed, while the threat of the Abyss was ever-present.

The ties between the three Noble Peoples weakened. The Elves became aloof and guarded, no longer willing to share their wisdom with former allies. The Dwarfs never trusted the Elves again, saying it was Elvish pride and sentiment that had doomed the world. The Primovantians were diminished by the conflict, some of the nobility of their spirit gone, and barbarities that had previously been unknown in their lands became commonplace. And yet cities were rebuilt, and civilisation made the slow crawl back to its previous heights.

Wars were frequent, as Orcs and Abyssals and other foul things plagued the land. More and more often Orcs came marauding from the north as the world cooled. The great Mammoth Steppes expanded in range, and land previously suitable to cultivation became uninhabitable.

The seas withdrew as they were taken up into the ice and the lands by their shores became poisoned by windblown salt, multitudes starving. Soon, the ice covered great tracts of Mantica, including the grand plains of Ardovikia, home to much of the latter-day glory of Primovantor, and the republic was slowly brought to its knees.

The last great war took place almost a thousand years ago. The cooling of the world was far from natural, and eventually the

Elven seers discerned that the goddess known simply as **Winter** was behind the chilling of Mantica. Somehow she had escaped Domivar's prison, or had not been cast down with the rest. Discovered, Winter fully unleashed her magic, and glaciers advanced like armies upon the civilised realms, strange creatures marching before them.

Men, Dwarfs and Elves stood shoulder to shoulder once more against the threat of the Wicked Ones. This time there was only one divine enemy, but all three peoples were far weaker than they once had been, and the aid of the Shining Ones could not be relied upon, for they too had lost a great deal of their power, and their minds had become unfocused, their actions whimsical.

For one hundred and fifty long years of seemingly unending cold, the war dragged on. Finally, Winter was confronted and bested in a battle of magic by Valandor the Great, the mightiest mage of his era. However, the culmination of this struggle against Winter wrought havoc upon the world. Even though they were victorious, the wisest Elves and Men could not foresee that the ending of Winter's Age of Ice would

drown so many lands under the thawing ocean, a last bitter gift to the world.

As the glaciers of Winter melted with magical rapidity, the sea came crashing back, and it did not stop once it had reached its original extent. The waters surged onward, inundating much of the lands of both Elves and Men. Valandor, the hero of the war, used his magic to hold back the waves, and although he managed to save vast swathes of the old lands, ultimately he was lost to the limitless power of the cold sea.

The Grand Republic of Primovantor was shattered forever, the northern provinces crushed under the ice, the colonnaded cities of the south empty of inhabitants now but for fish and kraken. Destroyed too was much of Elvenholme, the kindreds of the Elves scattered, the Sacred Groves of Elvenkind lost.

THE AGE OF CONFLICT

The world turns on, and a new age has begun – but it is an age of war. The ranks of the half-gods, both Shining Ones and Wicked Ones, are thinned, but they survive still, while the conflicts of the ancients have re-wrought the world time and again, offering fresh territories to Man, Dwarf and Elf alike. Some say this is a time of rebirth; if so, the midwives in attendance are war and strife.

Old oaths are broken, alliances forgotten. Where once the three Noble Peoples were united under the banners of vast empires, they now bicker and squabble, fighting between themselves and each other, carving meagre territories in lands plagued by violence and darkness. The Elven Kindreds no longer function as one kingdom, the glories of Primovantor are long gone, and the Dwarfs have hardened their hearts against the surface world. The threat of resurgent hordes of Orcs, Goblins, Ogres, and creatures of the Abyss is never far away, while armies of the dead pace the land, led by the necromancer Mhorgoth, who some say is the greatest threat Mantica has faced since the destruction of Winter.

MANTICA

BITTER LANDS

Tyris' Gate

Teiardon

Vale of Imlar

Valentica

Ice M

Great

Ardovikian Plain

Letharac

Dragon Teeth Mou

Dol Grago

Sathoi

PRIMO

SUCCESSOR KINGDOMS

The Endless Sea

N

Euhedral Library

Primant

Brokenwall Islands

Ruins of Vantoria

Port of Lantor

Drowned Republic

I

Northern Kindreds

Western Kindreds

Twilight Glades

Walldeep

Mountains of Alandar

Ileuthar

Easterr Reache

ELVENHOLME

Lethuia

Southern Kindreds

Frozen Sea

Skirnirak
Frontier Town

Zarak

ins

Ogre Lands

THE ABYSS

s of the Mammoth Steppe

Deiw

TRAGAR

st of
ahir

Cwl Gen

High Sea
of Bari

Halpi
Mountains

Mountain
of Kolosu

Gars

TOR

HEGEMONY
OF
BASILEA

Low Sea of Suan

Rhyn
Dufaris

The Great
Cataract

City of the
Golden Horn

za

Spartha

Sea of
Eriskos

Ruins of
Difetth

ABERCARR

Caeryn
Golloch

Keretia

Croguedd
Pass

Forsaken
Isles

Mountains of
Abkhazla

nt Sea

Southern Watchline

Straits
of Madness

Amaa-khopet

OPHIDIA

Hokh-man
(Serpent mouth)

Khotp
-remun

outh
Leith

Wastes of Ophidia

Khe-Luxarn

nderworld

The Cracked Land

MANTICA

THE INFANT SEA

Born of the melting ice at the end of the Winter War, the Infant Sea rushed in to drown the lands of men with terrifying rapidity. Once, the basin now occupied by that engulfing ocean was a fertile place, good cropland with many freshwater lakes at its centre. The bulk of the Republic of Primovantor, as well as many other kingdoms, was drowned under the Infant Sea's waters, only the northernmost regions and the mountainous province of Basilea surviving. A few islands are all that remain of once-mighty mountains, their peaks providing isolated pockets of land. Weather-worn statues and crumbled temples are all that remain of the people that once lived there. The Infant Sea is home to strange creatures, submarine races and terrible monsters. Trade routes crisscross the sea, linking together the cities and lands that surround it, but to sail these waters is not something to be done lightly.

THE CIVILISED LANDS

Much of the Infant Sea is surrounded by a jagged coastline of vast mountain ranges, the tallest and most famed of which is the Dragon's Teeth, which bound the entire north of the sea. In the foothills of the Dragon's Teeth, and along the narrow coastal plains at their feet, are to be found the majority of the realms of civilised Men. No longer governed by a Grand Republic, these realms, kingdoms, city-states, baronies and clans rise and fall on a daily basis, with new territory carved in battle, tenuous alliances forged, and entire cities wiped from the map by marauders.

The Empire of the Dwarfs occupies much of the east. The territories of the Elven Kindreds can be found to the southwest. The Hegemony of Basilea, the last true remnant of the Grand Republic of Primovantor, holds large swathes of the northeast, the Successor States bordering it to the northwest. Far to the south, across the Infant Sea, the coastline is rugged and barren, giving way quickly to baking deserts. The ancient Kingdom of

Ophidia lays claim to these arid territories. Everywhere between Basilea and Ophidia, smaller states, island kingdoms and independent cities are also to be found. The largest of these is Keretia, a large island, and home of the descendants of the last High Consuls of Primovantor, or so they say, a claim that sets them constantly at odds with the Hegemony of Basilea.

THE WILD

The majority of Mantica is wild and untamed. Many are the places that once held kingdoms or nations but which are now empty, with only ruins to testify to their passing. Other places – the deserts, the high peaks, the deepest forests, the steppes – have never been tamed.

The wilds of Mantica are dangerous and largely uncharted. What was once known about the world no longer holds true, for it has been made and remade time after time, and still bears the deep scars of the God War.

THE FORCES OF NATURE

Those venturing into the deep forests of Mantica say they feel they are being watched, and with good reason, for there is a force at work in the world that few – save the Elves – are aware of. The Sylvan Kin worship the Green Lady, a goddess of three aspects. Their lore has it that the Celestian known as the Green Lady did not split into a Wicked and Shining aspect when the Fenulian Mirror broke. With a supreme effort of will, she called upon the spirits of the trees and the beasts of the forests and they lent her their strength, and thus she kept herself together. Yet with the Celestians' power fragmented, she could not survive for long. To this end, she merged with Liliana, a Wicked One that had somehow retained a sense of morality and was tormented by it. The Lady of Nature then sought out Liliana's Shining side, and subsumed her too, bringing an uneasy peace to both parts. Thus the Lady is a goddess of two souls, and three aspects: Celestian, Shining and Wicked, and this perhaps explains the fickle yet balanced nature of the natural world.

All of nature yet untouched by evil magic in Mantica will respond to the Green Lady. The Sylvan Kin follow her unreservedly. Other, even more secretive creatures, serve her – centaurs, the eagles, and those wolves and bears that possess the power of reason. Elementals of the deep forest and stone are hers to command, the strange beings known as Tree Herders are among her most ardent servants. These creatures are locked in endless struggle against the despoliation of the natural world. Most often their foes are the Orcs and Goblins, but the logging camps of Men or the mines of the Dwarfs enrage them just as much.

Though the Elves of the Sylvan Kin worship the Green Lady as their goddess, they are too lost in their struggle for survival to be truly controlled by her. The Lady knows that her powers are limited to the wilds, and although she has eyes and ears everywhere in the form of fey creatures, birds, beasts and insects, she has long had need of servants capable of travelling the world independently, to

warn her of coming dangers, to predict the movements of enemies, and to understand fully the hearts of conquering warlords and brutish despoilers. To this end, the Lady enraptured a traveller, long ago, and inducted him into the mysteries of nature. It is said that this traveller was a Man of noble birth, a great warrior, who was so enamoured by the Lady's magic that he swore an oath to renounce his life of battle and serve the Green Lady for all eternity in peace. Thus was founded the ancient Order of Druids, and as their ranks have grown over the years, so has the Green Lady's influence.

Recruited largely from the lands of Men, who alone understand what it is to be possessed of both light and darkness, the Druids are solitary wanderers, who walk the length and breadth of Mantica, ever alert to threats against the balance of nature. If darkness threatens to overwhelm the forces of good in the world, the Druids summon the Lady's power to quell it. Yet they are ever mindful that should evil be driven back too far, the Lady will adopt the aspect of Liliana, and turn on the forces of good just as surely. Druids must, therefore, remain impartial in all things, lest their meddling cause great harm.

When summoned to war, the Lady is wrathful, having little love for either the evils of the Abyss, or for the smothering rectitude of the Shining Ones. The Sylvan Kin hold a hope that the Lady will restore balance to the world, reuniting the Shining Ones with their Wicked halves, bringing peace for the first time in thousands of years. This peace is itself to be feared, for it is the peace of the unsullied glade, of the untamed river. Should it come to pass, no city will remain.

THE ABYSS

Far to the northeast of the Infant Sea, amidst the shattered, soot-stained remnants of Winter's glaciers lies the greatest wound inflicted upon the world in the God War, a great pit in a land made ruinous by its presence, lit ruddy by lava aglow deep within. Here the last of the wicked gods reside, twenty-seven in number, their dark magic spewing ceaselessly into the world, twisting Men and nobler creatures into dark images of themselves.

A great rent in the ground, the Abyss is many miles deep, a fissure cleaved into the centre of the earth in past ages. A pall of smoke hangs above the Abyss, so that it and all the

Ba'el

Bane of the Mortal Kingdoms, Bringer of Woe, Eater of Realms. The Demon known as Ba'el has gone by many names in his long life. After the God War, he was one of the most prominent and powerful warlords of the Abyssal hordes, and his name was feared wherever it was spoken. Whole civilisations disappeared from the map under the unstoppable advance of his armies, rivers of blood and mountains of the dead the marks of his passing. Finally, he was brought low by the mighty hero known as Valandor, who bound him to an eternal prison beneath the ruins of the last civilisation he had razed – that of the Du'lan Var. Indeed, some secret cults in the darkest parts of the world whisper that Valandor could no sooner kill Ba'el than kill himself, for the two were inextricably bound together. In Basilea, such heresy is punishable by death; in Elvenholme, such talk will earn immediate exile. Whatever the truth, legend tells that Valandor intended to return and destroy Ba'el once he had righted the damage done by him, but the Great Flood claimed him before this could come to pass. Thus has Ba'el raged in his confinement for over a thousand years, sinking ever deeper into insane rage. If released, there will surely be no way of stopping him this time.

lands about it are shrouded in unnatural, perpetual night. These clouds of ash and soot are lit forever by the ruddy glow of fire, the beating heart of the earth, exposed to the cruel air. The Abyss is a terrible wound; a mortal wound, some say, one that has never healed and never will, and it bleeds. Plumes of molten rock spew in towering fountains into the sky. Poisonous smoke belches from the ground, hanging like a toxic miasma to choke any creature that strays unwittingly into it. Expanses of fine ash gather in hollows to drag down and suffocate the living. And always, the ground shakes and rumbles, opening fissures beneath the feet of the unwary.

This is the Abyss, the heart of all evil in the world. Often described in simple terms as a massive chasm in the world, the truth is somewhat stranger and far more insidious. When Domivar smote the ground with the mighty axe of Oskan he created a realm that was entirely otherworldly. Its dimensions are in constant flux, and cannot be thought of nor defined in simple terms like height depth, and breadth. The Abyss is a fiery and nightmarish other-space, existing parallel to the realms of the mortal races above. Its tendrils extend and contract underneath the world, and within its living, fluctuating boundaries, all manner of strange and unique things exist. It is a home and prison both for those evil gods cast down from heaven at the climax of the God War.

And yet, even here there is life. Up and down the cliffs that plunge to the molten lake at the Abyss' floor, cave mouths flicker with firelight, home to all manner of wicked, inhuman Abyssals. The air is alive with the sound of industry, screams, dark songs and, if one listens carefully, the insane cackling of the dark deities who dwell in the sinister depths. The foul legions who call this weird place home are many and varied, and yet all are born of flame. When they venture forth into the world above, nations tremble in fear.

Where great power and evil exist, those creatures dark of heart will surely follow. The greatest temple-citadels of the Abyssal Dwarfs rear high at either end of the Abyss, sentinel-mountains made of iron and brass and adorned with all manner of blasphemous carvings. Orcs dwell in great multitudes on the plains and in the mountains around it. Evil creatures prowl its hinterlands, heat-loving elementals slither in and out of its lava, and harpies hunt on the thermals that push up from its depths.

Men, Dwarfs and Elves are to be found here too. Slaves, in the main, dragged to the mines and foundries of the Abyss by raiding parties or in the aftermath of war. But there are others too, those that seek the black power of the evil gods for themselves, and they come willingly into the dark. Few indeed are those brave or foolhardy enough to explore the Abyss, and of those, fewer still are heard from again. It is said that any creature discovered trespassing within that twisted domain will be cursed to a hundred lifetimes of torment, becoming a crazed revenant in the service of the Abyssals.

The Mammoth Steppe

Winter's time may be long past, and her chill grip receded from the world, but at the poles Mantica is clad still in great caps of ice. Huge frozen cliffs of blue ice as tall as mountains stand sentinel over the world. By day they are visible for a hundred miles, by night the ice groans and roars. Some say this is Winter, that she lives still, and shouts her defiance at the warming sun once it has safely set.

At the feet of the ice cliffs are the Winterlands, the great plains of the Mammoth Steppe. An endless sea of dry grassland that circles the world, these plains are home to great beasts. Brutish horsemen thunder over it, following the herds, and Goblins ride their draft beasts pell-mell across its endless miles.

Men from more civilised lands venture here, too, to trade for pelts and mammoth ivory, but they are few in number and hardy. There are a few frontier towns upon the edges of the steppe, heavily fortified with log walls and bastions of permanently frozen earth, otherwise the signs of true civilisation are few. This is a hard land, and the people it breeds, of whatever species, are brutes.

The Ogres

There are few more brutish creatures than the nomadic Ogres, whose huge, mammoth-hide tents dot these plains. Ogres are large creatures, tribal and fierce, who migrate across the steppes in large caravans that are best avoided by any wanderer who doesn't wish to end up as supper. Though they believe that might makes right, and are aggressive in the extreme to outsiders, they are surprisingly intelligent, with a strange and complex social culture.

Their tribes are centred around powerful Warlocks – shamans who draw upon the power of the earth, the endless winds, and the immovable mountains. By dint of their communion with the mysterious Ogre gods, they alone can declare the successor of a tribal Warlord, granting him unnatural luck and fortitude in his coming trials.

Ogres are incredible hunters, possessed of great strength and stamina, and their intricate system of non-verbal communication makes them well-organised and efficient. These hunting practices are regularly pressed into service on Mantica's battlefields, for many Ogres regularly leave the Mammoth Steppes to serve as mercenaries in far-off armies. However, the call of the frozen north cannot be resisted forever, and all Ogres will eventually return to their tribe, where they will lend their strength to hunting massive beasts, or plundering remote settlements for whatever takes their fancy. Ogres are possessed of the unshakeable belief that anything that can be taken by force – which is most things, given their size and strength – is theirs by right. This frequently leads to battles against the nomadic Men of the plains, with whom they compete for game and trade goods. The horsemen are hardy and warlike, and numerous with it, thus their feud is set to never end.

Goblins, on the other hand, are seen as less of a challenge. The Ogres subjugated the Red Goblins of the Mammoth Steppes long ago, although for the most part the two races live alongside one another peaceably. The Goblins are seen as so weak that they are beneath the attentions of the average Ogre. However, long ago the Red Goblins learned that the only way to get their share of food and shelter on the inhospitable plains – and not get eaten by the many wandering beasts that live there – was to bow and scrape to the Ogres. Now they follow the Ogre hordes on the march, attending them as servants and often fighting alongside them. In return, the Goblins enjoy a measure of protection, as long as they stay out of the way of their lumbering overlords when they're in a belligerent mood; which is most of the time.

THE WINTERLANDS

The Winterlands are a frozen waste, long thought inimical to life. And yet rumours have begun to strike southwards of a small empire, carved from ice and rock, which holds sway over those chill lands.

Travellers to the north have reported that the Elves of the Ice Kindred have made a settlement in the Winterlands, but that is not entirely the case. These Elves are not the cold creatures of the Bitter Lands, but are instead vibrant and ambitious, drawn from the dispossessed and disenfranchised from across the Elven realms.

This young Kindred of Elves now rules over a city of ice, outcasts united under the banner of the exiled prince Talannar Icekin. It is said that Icekin used the last of his wealth to pay the Ogres to protect his newfound lands and construct his settlements, while his magic created a city of ice-spires, known simply as Chill, to watch over his domain. Hardy Northmen flock to his banner, as do strange elemental creatures of ice, and packs of vicious Snow Trolls. Warriors come from far and wide to swear fealty to this frozen prince, while his allegiance with the Ogres to the south adds to his strength. Icekin has somehow exerted his influence over disparate tribes and monstrous beasts, forging a Northern Alliance to be feared. If these rumours are true, then Icekin must have discovered something powerful in the frozen wastes, for the Elves swear that Prince Talannar was most unremarkable when he set out from Elvenholme, yet now seems bound for greatness.

THE ARDOVIKIAN PLAIN

After Winter's defeat, her ice retreated back to the pole of the north, and in the south up to the peaks of the Dragon's Teeth mountains. As this occurred, the Ardovikian plain was uncovered after ages pressed under cruel glaciers. Once home to the richest nine provinces of Primovantor, the ice had wiped it clean.

In the nine hundred years since the War with Winter, this plain has become hotly contested by all the peoples of Mantica and is once again rife with activity. The loess left by the glaciers is rich in nutrients. Young forests swathe large parts of it, surrounding the ancient greenwood of Galahir. Treasures from ancient times can be found in subterranean complexes, and the ice has eroded mountains, turning up many rich seams of ore. Here a Man – or a Dwarf, or an Elf – can make a name for himself.

THE SOUTHERN DESERTS

This expanse of arid desert is truly vast, stretching along most of the lower seaboard of the Infant Sea. Inexorably, day by day it advances, already it has devoured the realms of the Southern Elven Kindred, and much of the eastern plains. In many places, the dunes march unchallenged to the sea. The mysterious kingdom of Ophidia, sustained by its rich river valley, occupies much of the west, precious oases, desert cities and other, stranger kingdoms scattered across its interior. But beyond Ophidia, mysterious ruins, dead trees, and the bones of long-extinct creatures are all that challenge the whispering sand for space.

Further south are the Cracked Lands, a fractured landscape of parched stone and craters. Some sages maintain this was the site of a powerful kingdom, flattened by a falling comet during the God War, others that it is a site of evil to rival the Abyss.

Those of the Noble Races that have crossed the desert and ventured into the Cracked Lands are but a handful in number, for there is insufficient water to sustain a camel there. On the far side these travellers assert the land abruptly changes, becoming verdant and green, hills cloaked with jungle and teeming with life.

THE LANDS OF THE ELVES
Elvenholme

Winter's Final Gift, they call it, the sinking of much of Elvenholme under the raging sea, an inundation so swift and terrible it slew fully half of the Elven race. Once united, the Elves now coexist as an uneasy federation of interdependent kindreds, who pay but lip service to the Mage-Queen residing at the Twilight Glades.

The remaining members of the Western and Eastern Kindreds, inhabiting Elvenholme proper, still stand united. Those few who survive in the Northern Reaches remain aloof and look to their own affairs. To the very far north, the followers of the exiled prince Talannar Icekin have taken the newly revealed Winterlands as their own, and grow apart from what most Elves would regard as the true way.

Though bloodied, the Elves remain unbowed, and are slowly returning from the brink of extinction. Throughout the world's cities it is possible to find Elven quarters, where itinerant communities of dispossessed Elves have made their homes. Likewise, the Young Kingdoms are dotted with delicate Elven castles, the homes of those who have tired of the melancholy of the elder lands. Vital, ambitious and energetic, the Elves of the Young Kingdoms offer the greatest hope to all Elfkind.

The City of Walldeep

Therennia Adar is known commonly as Walldeep, so named for the great ring of rock that surrounds the city, protecting it from the sea which stands deep all about it. Raised by the heroic mage Valandor at the

time of the flood, and fortified still by old magic, the walls stand only forty feet above the wave-tops, yet plunge many hundreds to the city behind. Aside from the Brokenwall Islands, it is the last piece of the ancient heart of the Western Kindreds that exists today. Those that survive are known as the Sea Kindred now, and their ships skim the waves that cover their lands.

The Sea Elf soldiers who patrol the wall's parapets do so with sun on their faces, but behind those walls, the city itself lies in perpetual shadow. Walldeep is a powerful yet sad place. Only the Spire of Ages rises above the ring of stone into the light. The Spire of Ages is a holy site. Valandor the Great's broken form lies upon a couch of sea-ivory in a room at the very top. Time flows differently around the hero's corpse, which shows no sign of corruption, even after almost a thousand years. There are those who maintain that Valandor merely sleeps, and that when Therennia Adar and Elvenkind are once again threatened, he will rise up and ready himself for battle once more.

The Twilight Glades

The Elves who inhabit this most ancient of Elvish places mutter darkly that their time as a people is done, and that it was their kind's forsaking of tree and branch for stone and steel that brought them low. The Twilight Glades are the heart of Elven culture, the home of the High Marshall and the Mage-Queen and her court. Disunited they might be, but the Elves still heed to the Mage-Queen's words, and she is the closest they have to an overall leader.

The Twilight Glades lie at the centre of a range of hills on the southern shore of the Infant Sea. This is a magical realm woven into the forest. By uncertain roads one might reach the city of Ileuthar, a place like no other, grown from living trees. At its centre are the glades after which the entire kingdom takes its name. The Twilight Glades are a dense maze of ancient trees whose paths change constantly, and the deepest are unsafe for all but Mage-Queen Laraentha Silverbranch to tread.

These glades are but a faint shadow compared to those that once cloaked the slopes about Therennia Adar. Their lesser nature is a constant reminder to the Elves that they live at the twilight of their race, hence their name. Even so, great magic can be found in their dappled clearings and shadow-choked copses. Representatives of all the kindreds can be found in Ileuthar: city-merchants who dwell in the lands of men, Sea Elves, the nomadic Eastern Kindreds, dangerous Ice Elves, and even, it is rumoured, the envoys of the Twilight Kin.

It is hard for men to understand how such mortal enemies can sit and talk and share bread and wine, but Elves are not as men. Ileuthar is neutral ground for all Elves, and all of the Kindreds, no matter their attitudes to others, are welcome to the court.

Ileuthar and the Glades are especially beloved of the wild Sylvan Kin. Many of the Mage-Queen's attendants are drawn from their number, and it is they who convince the trees to take their useful shape through song.

The oldest trees in The Twilight Glades were seeded from the long-drowned world-tree itself, and it remains one of the most magically potent places on the planet. The walls between the layers of existence are thin in the Twilight Glades. At times of great need, the Elves will cross over through The Glade of Ways, a magical portal that is said to lead anywhere and everywhere. When they do so, they leave Mantica entirely, and walk the mysterious otherworldly roads called the Shadow Paths. This is perilous indeed, and not lightly done.

The source of the Elves' great magical power, the glades are coveted by many others, none more dangerous than Mhorgoth. Rumour has it that he dreams of seizing the Glades, opening their sorcerous portals and allowing the realms of the dead to mix freely with that of the living. Should this happen, the world would become a hellish place indeed, with Mhorgoth its fell king.

The Mountains of Alandar

West of the Twilight Glades, the peaks of Alandar rise dramatically, home to the dragons and their masters. The slopes of Alandar are covered in lush, warm forest, home to a stunning range of game, strange monsters, mysterious woodland denizens and dragons alike.

The Eastern Reaches

Where the mountains of Elvenholme meet the plains, the Elves of the Eastern Kindreds make their homes. In ages past, living among the rich life of the savannah gave these nomads an adventurousness of spirit and joy of being that made them renowned worldwide. But those days are done, replaced by dark times.

The savannah has been all but swallowed by the ever-expanding Ophidian Desert to the east, and the great beasts and Drakons that once roamed there are almost gone. Some of the Eastern Kindred have managed to retain fearsome Drakons, which they use as monstrous steeds in time of war. Though their numbers are few, and dwindling still, the strange symbiosis of Elf and Drakon is a sight to be feared in battle.

The Southern Kindreds

The Ophidian desert has already swallowed most of the lands of the Southern Kindreds, leaving but a few scattered cities alone in the sand, whose hinterlands, preserved by magic, are eaten away yard by yard as time marches on. These elves are hardy and stubborn, and their staunch defence of their ancestral territory has become legend among Elvenkind.

The Mouth of Leith

To the far east of Elvenholme, in the desert before one reaches Ophidia, lie the canyons of Leith. Deep and dark and verdant are these, ringing with the roars of creatures thought dead for aeons. Others live here too, the dark kin of the Elves, refugees from the times of the God War who have turned their backs on all that is divine in their bitterness. Rumour has it that they preside over a subterranean kingdom accessed only from the bottom-most canyons. Those that venture there uninvited do not return.

The Bitter Lands

The last lands before the Great Ocean, the Bitter Lands are a windswept, miserable place far to the Northwest. Savage seas surround them. They are cloaked in snow for six months of the year, lashed with freezing rains the rest. Ice smothers their northernmost reaches. In this inhospitable place the outcast Elven King Tyris Valellion makes his home. For two thousand years he and his clan have dwelt there, far from the light of Elvenholme, slowly transforming into a unique kindred in their own right – the Ice Elves.

They lived here even when Winter was at her height, surviving by taking her magic and turning it against her. The inhabitants of the Bitter Lands are pale and wan, their skin cold to the touch. They are masters of Ice Lore, and can summon up blizzards or storms of sharp-bladed hail on a whim.

A blade of ice a league across thrusts down from the far north, barring the land bridge that joins the Bitter Lands to the continent. This is Tyris' Gate. At his command, it will pull back with a chill groan fit to shatter the heavens. This makes the Bitter Lands an unassailable fortress. Should any enemy of the Elves make it over the seas or the ice, then they must deal with the ice-tipped spears and implacable hostility of the island's inhabitants, and their terrible storms.

Valandor the Great

A legendary figure whose origins are obscured in myth and legend, Valandor was the greatest Warrior Mage to ever walk the land, the father of magic to every one of the good races and claimed by each as their own, for in death, as in life, he is perceived by all who behold him as a shining exemplar of their own kind, his true form impossible to discern by even the strongest magics. Valandor was the champion of good for many centuries, and when he fell beneath the waters of the Great Flood, a light went out of the world.

There are some who believe that Valandor was a Celestian, sent to Mantica in mortal form as a last hope against Oskan's insane plans to destroy their race. Whatever the truth, Valandor is revered almost as a god far beyond Walldeep, and many Elves, Men and Dwarfs undertake long and hazardous pilgrimages to see his shrine. His name is invoked by warriors before battle, by wizards before deadly rituals, and by travellers set on dangerous roads.

If the legends are true and Valandor should one day return to the mortal realm, then surely the Age of War would end – it is this hope that fuels many soldiers who fight for righteous causes across Mantica.

The Forest of Galahir

Upon the Ardovikian plain north of the Dragon's Teeth Mountains, at the heart of those squabbling principalities called the Young Kingdoms, is the forest of Galahir. The trees here are the mightiest on all of Mantica, their trunks as thick and tall as any tower of stone built by Man, Elf or Dwarf. This is the home of the Sylvan Kin, and the centre of the power of the Green Lady. The Sylvan Kin have dwelt here since the dawn of Elven civilisation.

As the other kindreds grew further away from their roots, this Kindred embraced them. They would have nothing of the stone cities or the plains or the deserts and mountains their kin conquered, instead they remained where their ancestors had always dwelled. After the fall of the Celestians they became favourites of the Green Lady, and their magic helped keep her whole at the time of the sundering. Throughout the long flowering of Primovantor and the horrors of the God War, the Sylvan Kin remained here. Their forest has grown and shrunk and grown again, but its great heart has always remained.

When Ardovikia and the northern provinces of Primovantor were smothered in ice, the Sylvan Kin called upon the power of the Lady. Their realm was surrounded and isolated by the ice, but it was not crushed. For three hundred years the trees slept, bare of leaves, but they did not die. When Winter was defeated, the forest bloomed again, ready to bring life back to Ardovikia as the ice retreated.

The Brokenwall Islands

Strung across the mouth of the Infant Sea, the Brokenwall Islands are the last redoubts of the Sea Elves. Their elegant castles stand upon shining white cliffs, looking at the ocean in every direction. These are places of circling gulls, the crash of waves and the sigh of the wind. The salt tang is forever on the air, and the Sea Elves would have it no other way.

Elthenar Bladedancer

Elthenar Bladedancer is the youngest lord of the Eastern Kindred ever to have worn the mantle of rulership, yet in the decades since donning the sacred Helm of Dawn he has earned the respect of both ally and foe alike. Haughty, arrogant and proud, he is regarded as a fair if oft merciless and cold ruler, yet it is on the field of battle where his true skills come to the fore.

Elthenar's life has been one marred by tragedy, and indeed there are whispers that his bloodline carries with it a terrible curse. As a young child, he was orphaned after a night of darkness and bloodshed, his entire family slaughtered before his eyes. It is said that before that night he was a carefree child, full of laughter and light, but that all joy in him died that night, along with his family. Some whisper that it was that night that Elthenar learnt some terrible truth about his lineage, something that has tormented him ever since, but if there is any truth is such words, only Elthenar himself knows.

There is a darkness within Elthenar that has disturbed the Elders, an all-consuming desire for vengeance, a need of violence that is only barely kept in check. This is only unleashed in war, which he pursues with great vigour. He has led his armies to countless victories, many against overwhelming odds. Utterly fearless, he leads his armies from the fore, the deadly runesword Deathbringer in his hand. Only in the heart of battle, with the blood of the enemy flowing and the clash of swords deafening does he attain any sense of release from his torment.

THE LANDS OF THE DWARFS

The Golloch Empire

For many millennia the Dwarfs of Abercarr held themselves apart, content to hide in their halls while the ice pressed ineffectually down upon their mountain roofs. Only reluctantly did they agree to join the war against Winter, and have cursed the decision ever since. They lost many holds and more kin to the war, and once it was done, they turned their backs upon the shattered kingdoms of Elves and Men, retreated underground, and shut their mountain gates.

For ages insular, the long reign of King Golloch has turned the Dwarfs of Abkhazia outwards. In recent centuries, they have conquered land after land. Today, their empire stretches far into the little-known east, and knocks upon the very gates of Basilea to the west. Tenacious, hardy and determined, the Dwarfs have an unparalleled mastery of metal working, which they use to create marvellous artefacts and engines of war. A Dwarven army on the march is a glorious thing to behold, but terrible, for their approach means only war and subjugation.

Abercarr

Abercarr is large land buried by towering peaks. The bulk of it is a peninsula bounded to the north by the High Sea of Bari and the Low Sea of Suan, and to the south by the Infant Sea. The mountains are for the most part impassable and barren, their peaks cloaked in snow and glaciers, their shoulders forbidding, bare rock.

The Dwarfs have carved roads into and under the mountains, linking their vast cities with hidden, fertile valleys where they work the land. In places, entire mountains have been reformed to the Dwarfs' tastes, making them sculpted cities of living rock, their flanks aflame with the glow from hundreds of intricate windows. None of these holds is more impressive, nor as populous as Caeryn Golloch, the imperial capital.

To the east the mountains gradually dwindle to plains and forest. It is here that the Dwarfs have made most of their

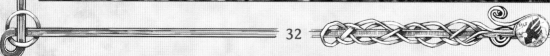

conquests, and the tunnels of the mountain people extend far out to these vassal cities and states. Rebellion is impossible when retribution lies under one's feet.

The west is a different story. The Dwarfs' realm abuts Basilea. In the time of Primovantor, the lands intersected with each other peaceably, the Dwarfs dwelling underground, and Men on the surface. Beneath the Plains of Diffeth, the ruins of Dolgarth, the Dwarfs' ancient capital, attest to this with their mix of mannish and Dwarven styles. But that was long ago. Dolgarth's halls were flooded when the ice receded, and they are now home to unspeakable horrors. Many adventurers brave the long dark of those Dwarf halls, lured by the promise of ancient treasure and forgotten lore, though few ever return.

Basilea has become increasingly hostile to the Imperial Dwarfs, seemingly at the insistence of their gods, and the land between the two civilisations is often contested, with Golloch's armies getting within cannon shot of the City of the Golden Horn's towering walls on two occasions. To the south, the mountains of Abkhazia

shelve abruptly to the northern reaches of Ophidia, and this border is heavily fortified. Along the Southern Watchline every peak is a redoubt. Subterranean roads wide enough for armies link every mountain-castle, lesser forts at three-mile intervals between. Gigantic runes of warding have been carved into the cliffs. Against what evil, the Dwarfs will not say.

The Great Cataract

Not all Dwarfs bend their knees to the might of Golloch. Over the Great Cataract that separates the High Sea of Bari and the Low Sea of Suan, the citadels of the Free Dwarfs and the Imperial Dwarfs glower at one another, the northern tower marking the southernmost limit of the lands of the Free Clans, many of whose number can also be found adventuring in the Young Kingdoms, while the southern tower stands sentinel over the border of Golloch's Empire.

The Great Cataract is an immense waterfall, so broad that it is only possible to see from side to side under very particular conditions. Here the High Sea of Bari thunders down a cliff three hundred feet high to join the Low Sea of Suan. The roar of the cataract is deafening. Around its edges Sirens play, cloaking their vile forms in glamours of beauty and allurement, luring the unwary to their dooms in the water of Bari or over the edge of the waterfall itself.

In the centre of the Cataract is Culloch Mor, a tree-cloaked rock topped by a simple altar of unknown origin. Here the Free Dwarfs and Imperial Dwarfs will come to treat, dragging themselves along the Chainway. The Chainway is the only direct way between the lands of the two Dwarf factions. A heavy chain that leads, rock to rock, from both shores to Culloch Mor, the Chainway allows ferries to traverse the very lip of the waterfall in safety. It is a spectacular if terrifying journey. As in the case of much Dwarf engineering, the Chainway is a marvel of the modern world.

The Free Dwarf Lands

After the God War, the Dwarfs expanded northwards, founding many new holds in the Halpi Mountains above the twin seas of Bari and Suan. The Halpi emanate outward in a large triangle from the Great Cataract,

Garrek Heavyhand

Garrek Heavyhand is a name known all around the Infant Sea, and it is not the only one he has. Sui Minuti – the Dwarf of a thousand tempers, the Elves call him, Garrek of the Hammer, the men of the squabbling states of Rim name him. Ostreoya Wiat – the eastern wind, as he is known to the savage horse tribes that roam the mammoth steppe. His exploits are legendary. Other names he has too: Traitor, Oathbreaker, Firequencher, Forge-slight and worse, for all Dwarfs loath the Heavyhands. No matter that Garrek has aided the Free Clans in their fight against the Orcs, or that he was the one who broke the Undead invasion of the Dwarf Empire, or that he was instrumental in brokering the fragile peace between the Free Clans and King Golloch.

Garrek may be guilty of many things, but he is innocent of the sins the northern Dwarfs hate him for. Garrek bears the dishonour of his clan, for the crimes his ancestor Gilgulli 'Goldless' Heavyhand committed. Dwarfs have long memories, and lack clemency, and Garrek suffers for it.

Five hundred and eighty three years ago, when the Dwarfs were still hiding in their halls and the expeditions into the ancestral north and west were just beginning, Gilgulli was a clan chief of modest means. Mocked for his lack of wealth, he conspired with unspeakable creatures to raid the royal treasure house of the high king, and made off with a great deal of loot. Among it, the Twenty-Seven God Boons, the most powerful magical artefacts ever fashioned in heaven, spoils of war from the long campaign against Winter millennia past. Gilgulli was discovered, as all thieves are, and the Heavyhand clan driven out. And yet the treasure was never recovered. Magic has a way of hiding itself when it wishes. The Twenty-Seven God Boons went into the world and vanished.

Born into poverty, Garrek has lived with this dishonour all his years. As a thin-stubbled youth he became disenchanted with his clan's acceptance of their fate, and swore an oath to recover the treasures and redeem them all. Since then he has fought side by side with Free and Imperial Dwarfs, drawing the ire of each when he has favoured one side over the other. But his fame has grown, and now, alongside his grizzled band of Heavyhand retainers, march many Dwarfs from all over the world, eager for adventure and gold.

In his right hand Garrek bears the Warp Hammer, the first of the Boons he discovered, upon his back the Cloak of Miph. Fifteen more of the magical treasures he has found or learned destroyed for all time; ten others he must gather before he can restore his family's honour.

If Garrek ever were to accomplish this monumental feat and not end his days dead at the hand or claw of some dread horror, there remains a problem: the artefacts came from the Royal Hoard before the Dwarven Civil War. Now the Hoard is the property of King Golloch. Returning the Boons there would earn him no favour from the northern Dwarfs, with whom he believes the Heavyhands belong. Worse, it would enhance the hungry king's might considerably.

Still, as Garrek himself would say "One thing at a time lad, one thing at a time."

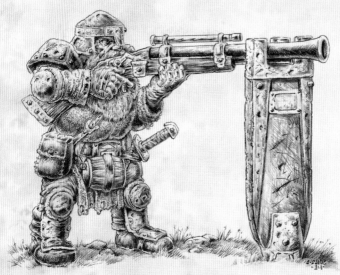

by Dwarfs fleeing from Golloch's tyranny (as they have it) and Dwarfs drawn from those communities scattered in the cities of Men. Like the Imperial Dwarfs, the Free Dwarfs are undergoing a period of expansion, but their conquests are their old holds. In the darkness under the Halpi mountains a war is being waged, as the Free Dwarfs attempt to expel the Orcs and Goblins who have taken up residence in their ruined homes.

and penetrate deep into the Mammoth Steppe. These mountains are rich in gems and ores, all things the Dwarfs love above all else, and the number of these holdings expanded rapidly as Dwarfs flocked north to exploit the riches of the mountains. They did not heed the warnings of the Warsmiths that the Halpis were dangerously close to the influences of the Abyss, which spits its evil into the world not far from the eastern slopes of the mountains.

The Northern Dwarfs scoffed, and a few braver souls even ventured into the dark lands that bound it where the very rarest metals may simply be picked up from the ground.

Under Winter's dark reign, the ice ground over the tops of the mountains, but the Dwarfs did not care. The Dwarfs of the north refused to answer the call of Elves and Men to war, bragging that ice could do them no harm in their mountain halls. It is perhaps fortunate that they did so, for Winter unleashed a surprise attack upon the northern Dwarfs. A tide of Abyssals, Orcs, and Goblins poured into their holds. Smaller and less well-defended than those of the south, many fell.

The Free Dwarfs come from the five holds that survived the fall of the north. Cwl Gen, Gars, Llyfanifeg, Marn and Rhyn Dufaris. Their numbers have been bolstered of late

Victory is far from assured, for evil things of immense power now dwell in the deep places of the world. Indeed, word spreads across the holds that one of the greatest kings of the Free Dwarfs, Thorrik Rockfist, has been slain by none other than the necromancer Mhorgoth, and that his city, Ironhold, built upon the banks of the Redgar River, is now a haunted place of shambling revenants and mournful spirits. If this is true, then the Free Dwarfs are in dire peril, attacked from all quarters by Orcs, Abyssal Dwarfs and Undead, with not even their Imperial kin to call upon for aid.

Tragar

What became of the northern Dwarfs who had established mining communities around the Abyss was not to be discovered until hundreds of years later. Drawn there by the promise of riches, these once noble-hearted creatures were twisted by the dark whispers of the Father of Lies. Now their hellish industries surround the Abyss. Their cities stand at either end – Zarak and Deiw – bywords for evil and pain. They call their kingdom Tragar, and all fear it.

The smoke of the Abyss chokes the air, the ruddy light of the fires in its depths make it impossible to tell if it is night or day. The air rings with the sounds of

Fire Magic

Fulgria, Goddess of White Fire, is among the chief deities of the Dwarfs, it is to her that the Dwarf Warsmiths appeal when working their craft, for her volcanic power is drawn from the heart of the earth and as such she has great affinity with the Dwarf race.

With her blessing, a Dwarf Warsmith can forge mighty weapons indeed. All the gods possess a positive and a negative aspect, good and evil facets of what is truly one being. The dark sister of Fulgria is Ariagful, and while the Dwarf Warsmiths offer prayers to Fulgria, the Ironcasters of the Abyssal Dwarfs go a step further, harnessing the magic of Ariagful in violent feats of sorcery.

Even within the Free Dwarf Clans, dark rumours are whispered of King Golloch, that his success in matters of war is surely due in part to his religious devotion not to the Shining One Fulgria, but to Ariagful.

the Abyssal Dwarf's industries and the screams of their slaves. Thousands are sacrificed daily, pushed from the Gift-Piers of Zarak and Deiw, long stone arches that end high above the broil of the pit. All for the greater glory of Oskan and his twenty-six Abyssal Lords.

Day and night the fires of industry burn bright, and instruments of war are churned from great forges on a scale never before seen. The self-proclaimed Overking of the Abyssal Dwarfs, Zerkziz of Zarak, is consumed by a desire to destroy his former kin. He looks to the burgeoning kingdom of Golloch, and wishes nothing more than the subjugation of every Dwarf who serves him. But to reach Abercarr, Zerkziz must first destroy the Free Dwarfs that stand in his way. With their holds under his command, his armies would surely swell beyond measure, and the lands to the south would be his to conquer.

THE LANDS OF MEN

Primovantor

The Grand Republic of Primovantor was the greatest civilisation Mantica had seen, at its height covering a third of the known world. The time of Primovantor was one of high art and high science, a beacon of hope against the relentless chill of Winter's Age of Ice, the last era of the God War. It was the High Consul of the Primovantians who urged the ending of Winter, and thus sealed the fate of his own land. Most of Primovantor that was not ruined in the war was drowned under the Infant Sea. The holy city of Primantor itself survived. The city is now mostly ruinous, trees fill its wide boulevards, and the inhabited parts are little more than villages, divided by a wilderness of crumbling masonry.

Some of the glory of Primovantor did survive, in Basilea, the Eastern portion of the Republic. Basilea persists to this day, albeit in much diminished form and certainly not as a republic, but as the hidebound Hegemony.

The Successor Kingdoms

The High Consul dead, much of the land laid waste, the shock of the inundation was the final blow to the tottering Republic. The remnants of it broke up into warring statelets, and much was forgotten. Dozens of independent city states now rule small kingdoms all over the peninsula

of Primovantia, and at the feet of the Dragon's Teeth to the north and west. The greatest of them all is Valentica, which occupies the entirety of the lands bearing the same name.

The people here are great traders, keen-eyed sailors with a thirst for adventure, and hold close ties with the Sea Elves. Also of note is the mountain duchy of Sathoi, a provider of skilled mercenary companies, and the city-state of Geneza, another sea nation of traders, and great rivals of both the Valenticans and Sea Kindred. Geneza is unique in that it is built atop the ruins of an earlier city, drowned by the sea. Unable to escape, the Genezans simply built upwards, and modern Geneza sits upon the waves like a stone ship. Primovantor itself persists as one of these states, although it is greatly shrunk in size, its inhabited portions are like villages surrounded by a harsh wilderness of broken stone and briars.

For the main part small and individually weak, it is these same kingdoms now that see the flowerings of rebirth. For many years little more than barbarian realms, the city states, dukedoms and petty principalities of the coast and mountains have reached fresh levels of understanding, while art and science once again flourish. Over the mountains to the north, realms expand and new countries are born from the virgin lands of the Young Kingdoms, often with the Men of the Successor Kingdoms as their founders.

The Hegemony of Basilea

Conservative by nature and paralysed by ritual it may be, but Basilea still reflects some of the ancient glories of Primovantor. Its cities are the largest, its princes the richest, its mages the most powerful of all the kingdoms of Men. Basilea insists that it is the only true protector of Primovantor's legacy. Temples are still maintained to the long-gone Celestians in Basilea, while the worship of their good aspects, the Shining Ones, is an integral part of life.

It is a kingdom where time has stood still, where some of the glories of the elder days might still be found. Noble Paladins devote their entire lives to battle and prayer,

undergoing arduous quests to prove their purity to the Shining Ones. Many Orders of the Sisterhood guard the borders. Purity, courage, and strength are the watchwords of these warrior virgins.

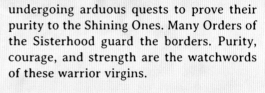

The Hegemon is king and high priest both. It is within his power to appeal directly to the Shining Ones. These remaining noble aspects of the Celestians dwell atop the mountain of Kolosu, an impossibly high pillar of rock, and from there they watch over the Hegemony.

They rarely manifest directly, although it is not unknown for one or the other of them to take to the battlefield even in these lesser times, but will send their servants to the aid of the Basilean armies, should the occasion warrant it. These are the Elohi, angelic beings of immense power, who appear in the guise of beautiful, winged humans armoured all in gold. In war they are all but unstoppable, as terrible in combat as they are merciful and kind out of it.

But alongside the purest aspect of true faith and benevolence, Basilea has its sinister side too. Free thinking of any kind is not easily tolerated, and Basilean culture therefore remains hidebound and unchanging. Periodic panics about agents of the Wicked Ones sweep the nation, leading to innocent and guilty alike being condemned to death by mass drowning in the Cleansing Pools.

The Hegemon does not rule unchallenged; blood feud is all too common, driven by fires of honour and religious fervour that cannot be quenched. Orcs press upon Basilea from the north, while relations with the Dwarfs to the east are at their lowest ebb.

And atop their pillar of stone, the Shining Ones watch, for the most part silent. Protectors of Mankind, some say, capricious immortals who toy with the lives of lesser beings, say others.

The City of the Golden Horn

Largest and most spectacular of all of the cities of Men, the City of the Golden Horn is the capital of Basilea. Over a millions citizens live within its precincts according to the Royal Census, and the true figure is likely to be much higher. The Golden Horn is a promontory projecting into the Sea of Eriskos. The city was built in ancient times upon the eastern bank of what was once a broad river canyon, now lapped by the sea, and has grown so huge it covers both shores. It is the crossroads of the world. Men of all nations can be found there, merchants from every sea, and sellswords from every land.

The Golden Horn is the home of the Hegemon, and his palace rises majestically from the warren of streets around it. Here too are the greatest temples to the Celestians and the Shining Ones, the Universities of Magic, the Duma of Nobility, and many other important parts of the state apparatus. It is said a man may buy anything in the Golden Horn. Trade extends deep into the intrigues of the Hegemonic Court, and this saying knowingly includes the fates of kingdoms.

The Golden Horn is home both to squalor and beauty, to cruelty and mercy. Man in all his great variety walks its streets, as do Elves, Dwarfs, and other races. Protected behind three rows of thick walls of increasing height, studded with hundreds of brazen cannon, the city is an impregnable fortress and has never fallen. The Golden Horn, however, occupies land that King Golloch of the Dwarfs claims as his own, so perhaps this fine record will not go untarnished for much longer.

The Young Kingdoms

Upon the Ardovikian plain, new nations are being born. From the Dragon's Teeth in the south to the edge of the Mammoth Steppes, hundreds of small kingdoms, independent townsteads, isolated keeps and fortified manses have been established, each one alternately warring and allying with its neighbours. The majority are ruled by Men, although there are realms of all kinds to be found, from Dwarfs and Elves to even – it is whispered – Vampires.

After nine centuries, some are only now showing promise, absorbing others through treaty or conflict, and becoming players on the grander stage. Cruel tyrants, idealistic nobles, religious zealots, chancers, pauper-kings, outcast knights, sorcerers and mercenaries – many and more have attempted to carve out a kingdom here, by the strength of their steel or the depths of their cunning. Some few have been so successful that they even now look beyond the Young Kingdoms, dreaming of the day that they may conquer those lands and march across the Dragon's Teeth to Primovantor at the head of an unstoppable army.

The wise see the powers of the future taking root upon the Ardovikian flatlands, yet for now it remains a rough land, full of promise and danger. To be a king here is hard, but then again, here anyone can become a king.

The Black Pass Legacy

It is not only Men who rule in the Young Kingdoms. Indeed, one of the largest battles ever fought there, at an accursed maze of canyons known as the Knife Spires, was contested between Elves and Dwarfs.

The feud between the Dwarf Ironhelm clan and the Elven free city of Prince Nuadalor has raged for more than three centuries, beginning when the Dwarf lord, Balor Ironhelm III slew the Elf King Celebor Swiftsword at Borghan Ridge for some perceived slight, thus consigning the Elves to many years of decline. When Celebor's son, Prince Nualador, came of age, he swore vengeance on the Dwarfs, and began the long process of rebuilding his city, and his army.

Baiting the Dwarfs into marching against him at the Knife Spires, Prince Nualador delivered a masterful ambush against Balor Ironhelm at the Battle of Black Pass, which resulted in the deaths of ten thousand Dwarf warriors, including the old lord himself. The Elves, as a result, have become one of the most feared powers in the Young Kingdoms. The Dwarfs, almost destroyed by the battle, have locked themselves away in their mines, where the son of Balor, Halfi Ironhelm, plots his revenge.

Whether it comes in a month, a year, or a century, the Dwarves will not let the slaughter of their people go unpunished, and the feud shows no signs of ending.

Ophidia

Ancient Ophidia, the most venerable of all man's realms, has weathered catastrophe and war implacably. Long the rival of Primovantor, it has survived from the ancient time of light until today. For more than ten thousand years the God-Kings have watched over their subjects, who toil as they ever have on the perilously thin green strip of fertile land adjoining the River Ophid.

Ophidia is a harsh land, of ritual and cruelty, but also of beauty and opportunity, of gold and mystery. Its nobility are sorcerers, demonologists and even necromancers, though many whisper that its true masters are anything but human. It is a place where adventurers can find their fortune, braving serpent-haunted tombs and ancient ruins. Assassins lurk in every shadow, alchemists ply their trade in vast painted markets, and women of enviable beauty dance the long nights away to the hypnotic sound of drums.

In crumbling temples and golden towers, the cult of the Magi make pacts with demonic Djinn in exchange for wealth and near-immortality. From this source, the Magi draw magical powers the envy of other realms of Men, but they do so at a cost to their souls that few would be willing to pay. It is only the wisdom of the Elven Southern Kindreds that allows the Magi to tread the fine line between arcane mastery and damnation, and this pact between Men and Elves is a rare thing in these troubled times.

It is a hard truth that much evil in the world has come from Ophidia: the necromantic art of death magic, unbound Abyssals and those terrible perversions of humanity: the vampires and the ghouls, ghastly by-products of the Ophidian Sorcerers' never-ending quest for immortality. This is a land where desert-borne spirits are enslaved to raise the monuments of the God-Kings, where elaborate funerary rituals are essential to prevent the return of the dead, where proud warriors fight alongside their reanimated fallen ancestors, and where, at the heart of it all, the true, cold-blooded Ophidians plot and scheme from their glittering towers.

O Mighty Dead!

Hassim staggered into the ancient tomb, clutching his shoulder, from which half an arrow still jutted.

"My lord!" Hassim gasped. "The vanguard is slain and the left flank crumbles. The Orcs are too many — give the command, and I shall sound the retreat."

The Magi, cloaked in robes of black and crimson, appeared not to hear the captain of the guard. Instead, he traced his fingers across a panel of etched gold upon a stone altar, muttering strange incantations. "Have faith, captain," he said at last, "the Orcs will not overrun us."

"But…" Hassim tried to protest, then stopped abruptly as a strange rumbling sound echoed through the ancient chamber. He turned to face the baking sun outside, thinking that the Orcs had unleashed some new devilry upon his forces, before realising that the sound came from beneath them. From the catacombs.

"Follow me, Hassim," said the Magi, striding past the captain and into the Ophidian desert.

Everywhere, hulking desert Orcs tore into Hassim's guardsmen. The Magi did not stop — he clambered atop a stone dais upon the side of the temple, even as the monument shook, and raised his golden staff to the sun.

"O Mighty Dead!" he shouted at the heavens. "I, Bithisar Ab Jarriah, Magi of Ushanta, Keeper of the Sacred Scrolls of Djiretta, command thee rise!"

Stone slabs hidden beneath the sand began to slide apart, revealing a huge black vault. And from its depths marched the old ones, the Eternal Guard. Rank after rank filed from the darkness, their bronze armour gleaming, death-masks hiding wasted visages. They formed up into disciplined regiments, hundreds strong, a wall of bronze, steel and bone awaiting the command of the Magi.

"As I said, Hassim," said the Magi, "the Orcs will not overrun us. Not today."

THE RULES

UNITS

In *Kings of War*, all units are made up of one or more models. The number of models that make up a unit is specified in each unit's stats (explained on page 51), and will normally correspond to the number of models you get in boxes supplied by Mantic. These models must be glued onto bases and formed up into units as described below. Each unit belongs to one of the following Types.

Infantry (Inf)

Infantry units come in four sizes:

• Troops consisting of 10 models, arranged five models wide in two ranks.

• Regiments consisting of 20 models, arranged five models wide in four ranks.

• Hordes consisting of 40 models, arranged ten models wide in four ranks.

• Legions consisting of 60 models, arranged ten models wide in six ranks.

Cavalry (Cav)

Cavalry units come in three sizes;

• Troops consisting of 5 models, arranged in a single rank of five.

• Regiments consisting of 10 models, arranged five models wide in two ranks.

• Hordes consisting of 20 models, arranged ten models wide in two ranks.

Large Infantry (Lrg Inf) & Large Cavalry (Lrg Cav)

Large Infantry and Large Cavalry units come in three sizes:

• Regiments consisting of 3 models, arranged in a single rank of three.

• Hordes consisting of 6 models, arranged in two ranks of three models.

• Legions consisting of 12 models, arranged in two ranks of six models.

War Engines (War Eng)

A War Engine is a unit consisting of a single war machine, like a catapult or a bolt thrower. It may also have number of crew models, but these are purely decorative and should be arranged around the machine in a suitably entertaining fashion.

Since the crew is merely decorative, they are ignored for all in-game purposes, such as checking ranges, movement etc.

Monsters (Mon)

A Monster is a unit consisting of a single model – a large and powerful mythical beast or magical construct.

Heroes (Hero/xxx)

A Hero is a unit consisting of a single model. It can be an officer, a sorcerer or even a mighty lord of its race. Heroes vary in size between different races, and can ride many types of mount or even monstrous war-beast, so Heroes always have a tag in bracket specifying what type of unit they belong to – which helps with determining their height and other special rules that are related with certain units.

So a Hero could be a (Hero/Inf), or a (Hero/Cav), or a (Hero/Mon), or a (Hero/Lrg Inf), or a (Hero/Lrg Cav), and though we have not yet conceived a (Hero/War Eng), one never knows...

Sometimes Heroes have options that allow them to choose different mounts – if a mount is chosen, the Hero's unit type will of course change to that of the relative mount, as specified in the Hero's entry.

Base Sizes

Infantry models are based on 20mm square bases, apart from some that will be marked as exceptions in their entry (such as Orcs, which are on 25mm square bases).

Large Infantry models are based on 40mm square bases, apart from some that will be marked as exceptions in their entry (such as Lesser Obsidian Golems, which are on 50mm square bases).

Cavalry models are based on 25x50mm.

Large Cavalry models are based on 50mm square bases, apart from some that will be marked as exceptions in their entry (such as Chariots, which are on 50x100mm).

Monsters and War Engine models are based on 50mm square bases.

Heroes fit on the relevant base of their type unless specified otherwise. For example, a Hero (Inf) will be on a 20mm square base (except for Orc Heroes, which are on 25mm square bases), a Hero (Cav) will be on a 25x50mm base, etc.

Exceptional Base Sizes
You may need a wider or deeper base for exceptionally large heroes, monsters or war engines – in such rare cases, use the smallest base that you can fit your model on.

FRONT, REAR, FLANK

Normally in *Kings of War*, units have four facings: front, rear, left flank and right flank. Each of these facings possesses an 'arc', an area determined by drawing imaginary lines at 45 degree angles from each corner of the unit, as shown in Diagram A.

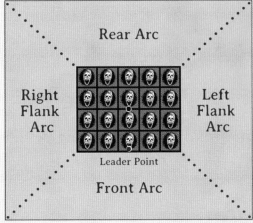

Diagram A – Front, Rear, Flank

UNIT LEADER POINT

The unit leader point is the exact centre of the front edge of a unit's base. The reason why we call it 'leader point' is that some players like to place a suitably imposing model in the centre of the first rank to 'lead' the unit.

Whenever the rules say to take something 'from the unit leader point' (or just 'from the unit leader'), such as a measurement or line of sight, it is from this point in the exact centre of the unit's front edge.

Common Unit Base Sizes

Unit Type	Base Size	Troop	Regiment	Horde	Legion
Infantry	20x20mm	100x40mm	100x80mm	200x80mm	200x120mm
Infantry	25x25mm	125x50mm	125x100mm	250x100mm	250x150mm
Cavalry	25x50mm	125x50mm	125x100mm	250x100mm	n/a
Large Infantry	40x40mm	n/a	120x40mm	120x80mm	240x80mm
Large Cavalry	50x50mm	n/a	150x50mm	150x100mm	300x100mm
Large Cavalry	50x100mm	n/a	150x100mm	150x200mm	300x200mm

CAN THEY SEE?

During the game, you will at times need to determine whether one of your units can see another one, normally an enemy unit that your unit intends to charge or shoot.

Arc of Sight

First, we'll assume that your unit can only see things that are at least partially in its front arc – its 'arc of sight'. The flank and rear arcs are completely blind.

Line of Sight (LOS)

Of course, terrain and other units can still get in the way and hide targets that are in your unit's arc of sight. To determine whether your unit can actually see a target that is in its arc of sight, follow the rules below.

Unit Height
Each unit has a height assigned according to its type:

Unit Type	Height
Infantry	1
Large Infantry	2
Cavalry	2
Large Cavalry	3
Monsters	4
War Engines	1

A hero's height is equal to that of its type. For example, a Hero (Inf) will have a height of 1, while a Hero (Cav) will have a height of 2.

Some units may be an exception and have a different height – this will be specified in their entry (e.g. Orclings are height 0).

Drawing LOS
To determine line of sight, draw an imaginary straight line from the unit leader point to any point of its target's base. If this imaginary line passes over no other unit's base or terrain features, then line of sight is not blocked.

If either your unit or the target unit are taller than any other units or terrain in the way, then line of sight is not blocked. If any units or terrain in the way are the same height or taller than both your unit and the target unit, then line of sight is blocked.

Note that the line of sight does not have to be the shortest line between your unit leader point and the target unit's base; any line from your unit leader point to any part of the target unit's base will do fine.

If you're unsure whether your unit can see a target unit or not, roll a die. On a 4+ it can see it, on 3 or less it cannot.

Terrain and LOS
This is discussed in more detail on page 59.

MEASURING DISTANCES

You can measure any distance at any time you like. Unless otherwise specified, the distance between two units is the distance between the two nearest points of the units' bases.

Keep Your Distance!

In order to avoid confusion, keep your units at least 1" away from enemy units at all times, except when charging or regrouping as explained later. To remove any confusion, ensure that your units are not in base contact with other friendly units at all times.

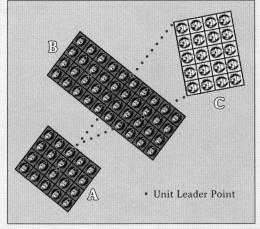

Diagram B1

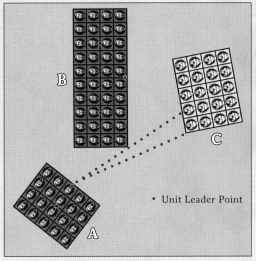

Diagram B2

Drawing Line of Sight – Example A

Unit A is trying to draw line of sight to Unit C (see Diagram B1). The dotted line represents the line of sight trying to be drawn. If either Unit A or Unit C are taller than Unit B then line of sight is NOT blocked. If Unit B is the same height or taller than both Unit A and Unit C then line of sight is blocked.

Drawing Line of Sight – Example B

In this example (see Diagram B2), Unit B is considered to be as tall as Units A and C and therefore blocks line of sight. Unit A can still see Unit C by looking around the edge of Unit B.

STATS

Each unit in *Kings of War* has a name and a series of statistics (for short, we call them 'stats'), which define how powerful it is in the game. These are:

- **Type.** Whether the unit is Infantry, Cavalry, etc.

- **Unit Size.** How many models the unit comprises of.

- **Speed (Sp).** How fast the unit moves, in inches.

- **Melee (Me).** The score needed by the unit to hit in melee.

- **Ranged (Ra).** The score needed by the unit to hit with ranged attacks. If it has no normal ranged attacks, this is a '–'.

- **Defence (De).** The score the enemy requires to damage the unit.

- **Attacks (Att).** The number of dice the unit rolls when attacking, both at range and in melee.

- **Nerve (Ne).** A combination of the unit's size and its training and discipline, this stat shows how resistant it is to damage suffered.

- **Points (Pts).** How valuable the unit is. Used for picking a force and often for working out victory points, depending on the scenario used.

- **Special.** Any special equipment (like ranged weapons) and rules the unit has.

Example:

Kindred Archers							Infantry
Unit Size	Sp	Me	Ra	De	Att	Ne	Pts
Troop (10)	6	5+	4+	4+	8	10/12	115
Regiment (20)	6	5+	4+	4+	10	14/16	150
Horde (40)	6	5+	4+	4+	20	21/23	250
Special: *Bows*							

THE TURN

Much like chess, *Kings of War* is played in turns. Just roll a die to decide who is going to have the first turn – the player winning the die roll decides who goes first. That player moves, shoots and strikes blows in close combat with their units – this concludes Turn 1 of the game. After that, the opposing player takes a turn – Turn 2 of the game, and then the players keep alternating this way until an agreed time limit or turn limit is reached.

A player goes through the following three phases in their turn:

1) Move phase;
2) Shoot phase;
3) Melee phase.

We'll examine each of these phases in detail on the following pages.

Dice

In these rules, whenever we refer to a die or dice, we mean a normal six-sided die, which we call D6. Sometimes we also use terms like 'D3', which is the result of a D6 divided by 2 (rounding up), or 'D6+1', meaning rolling a D6 and adding 1 to the result, or 2D6, which is rolling two dice and adding them together.

Re-Rolls

When you are allowed a re-roll, simply pick up the number of dice you are allowed to re-roll and roll them again. The second result stands, even if it's worse than the first. Regardless of the number of special rules that apply to a particular circumstance, you can never re-roll a re-roll, the second roll always stands.

MOVE

During the Move phase of your turn, pick each of your units in turn and give them one of the following orders:

Halt!
The unit does not move at all.

Change Facing!
The unit remains stationary and can pivot around its centre to face any direction. See Diagram C.

Advance!
The unit can advance straight forward up to a number of inches equal to its Speed. At any point during this move (i.e. before or after advancing, or anywhere along its advance), the unit can also make a single pivot around its centre of up to 90 degrees from its original facing. See Diagram D.

Back!
The unit can move straight backwards at up to half of its Speed. See Diagram E.

Sidestep!
The unit can move sideways straight to its left or straight to its right at up to half of its Speed. See Diagram E.

At the Double!
The unit can advance straight forward up to double its Speed. See Diagram E.

Charge!
This is by far the most exciting of orders. It is also the most complicated and so it's described in detail below.

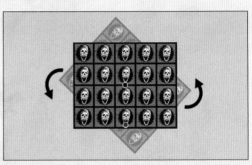

Diagram C – Change Facing

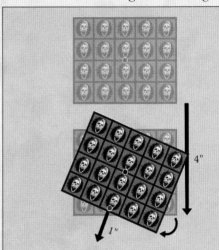

This Skeleton regiment has a Speed of 5" and it's ordered to Advance! first, it's moved 4" straight forward, then it's pivoted around its centre, and finally it completes its advance by moving a futher 1" straight forward.

Diagram D – Advance!

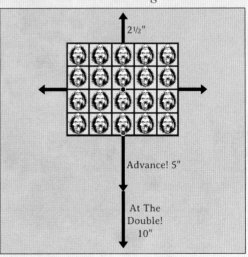

Diagram E – Move

UNIT INTERPENETRATION

Interpenetration When Moving

The following rules regulate inter-penetration when a units moves directly forward, backwards or sideways.

Friends

Friendly units can be moved through (except when charging, see below), but you cannot end a unit's move on top of another unit, so you'll have to be sure that your units have enough movement to end up clear of their friends.

Also, at the end of their move, your units must not be in base contact friendly units. This ensures that both you and your opponent can clearly tell them apart.

Enemies

Enemy units, on the other hand, block movement. Your units can never approach to within 1" of them, except when charging or during a pivot.

Interpenetration When Pivoting

In reality, regimented units are more flexible in rearranging their ranks and files than our miniatures, so when a unit is pivoting around its centre it can pivot through both friends and enemy units, and all types of terrain, including blocking terrain and the edge of the table. They must of course still end their pivot (and their entire move) clear of blocking terrain (and completely on the table!), not in base contact with friendly units, and 1" away from enemy units.

CHARGE!

A charge is the only way your units can move into contact with the enemy. A unit can charge a single enemy unit ('the target') as long as the following conditions are met:

- the target is at least partially in your unit's front arc;

- the unit can see the target;

- the distance between your unit's Leader point and the closest point of the target unit's base is equal to or less than double your unit's Speed;

- there is enough space for your unit to physically move into contact with the target by moving as described below.

Moving Chargers

As they move, charging units can move forward without measuring how much distance they actually cover, and pivot once around their centre up to 90°, at any point during their move.

They must, however, always use the shortest way possible, going around any blocking terrain and any unit in their way (friends and foes). Note that they must go through any area of difficult terrain or obstacle that would normally slow down their movement. These elements of terrain do not slow down Charge moves, but they cause the charging unit to suffer a slight penalty in the ensuing melee.

Once the charging unit is in contact with the target, align it with the side of the target you are charging so that it is flush with it.

Finally, shuffle the chargers sideways until their unit leader point is facing directly opposite the centre of the target unit, or as close as possible to it.

Basically, the main thing that matters during a Charge move is that the unit has physically enough space to move into contact with the target. Note that the unit needs to be able to have at least some of its front physically into contact with the unit being charged, contacting a unit exclusively with the point in the exact corner of the unit is not allowed.

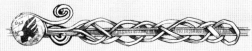

Flank and Rear Charges

If the leader point of the charging unit is in the target's front arc when the order to Charge is given, the unit must charge the target's front facing.

If the leader point of the charging unit is in the target's right or left flank arc when the order to Charge is given, the unit **must** charge the target's appropriate flank facing.

If the leader point of the charging unit is in the target's rear arc when the order to Charge is given, the unit **must** charge the target's rear facing. See Diagram F.

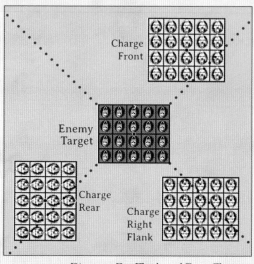

Diagram F – Flank and Rear Charges

Proximity to Enemies

Remember that when charging, units don't have to stay 1" away from enemies, and this means that sometimes a charging unit may end up in contact with both its target and one or more enemy units it has not charged (e.g. when charging a unit that is part of a tight enemy battle line). In this case, you'll have to nudge these enemy units away to ensure that they are no longer touching.

This represents the charging unit concentrating its fighting efforts against a single enemy, while holding at bay the other enemy units nearby. It might look a bit strange at first, but remember that the enemy units will normally get to charge back into the fight to help their friends in their following turn.

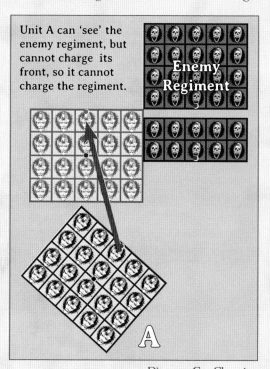

Unit A can 'see' the enemy regiment, but cannot charge its front, so it cannot charge the regiment.

Diagram G – Charging

Corner-to-Corner Charges

In some rare cases, the only possible way for a charger to make physical contact with a target would be by literally having one corner of its frontage in contact with one corner of the target.

These extreme cases are called 'corner to corner' contact – one example of this is shown in Diagram G.

We deem that this is not enough to warrant a sensible charge and combat, so we disallow these charges.

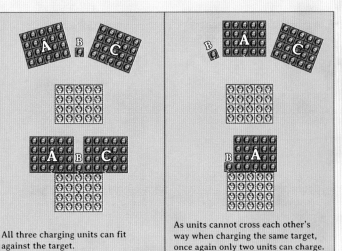

The target is only wide enough for two units among A, B and C to charge. The player chooses B and C.

All three charging units can fit against the target.

As units cannot cross each other's way when charging the same target, once again only two units can charge. The player chooses B and A.

Diagram H – Multiple Charges

Multiple Charges Against the Same Target

If two or more of your units are able to charge the same enemy unit, they can do so, as long as they can fit. Just issue a simultaneous order to all of the units that are charging the same target.

Any units that have charged the same facing of the target will have to share the space available as equally as possible, as long as they can fit after all chargers have moved.

If there isn't enough space for all of the units to fit against the facing of the target they are charging, some of the units will not charge and must be given a different order.

You will notice how it is impossible for three units of exactly the same frontage (e.g. 100mm) to charge the facing of an enemy that has the same width (100mm). This is because corner-to-corner charges are not allowed – so only two such units can charge the same facing, the third will have to be given a different order.

Also note that, in multiple charges, charging units cannot cross each other's way in (see the last example of Diagram H).

Counter Charge

If a unit was charged by one or more enemy units in the previous turn, it may elect to perform a Counter-Charge instead of a regular Charge.

If a unit decides to Counter-Charge then it may only do so against an enemy unit which charged it in the previous turn. It does not need Line of Sight and the enemy unit does not need to be in the front arc, so it may Counter-Charge against units in its flank or rear arcs.

Rather than making a normal Charge move, the unit simply pivots to face the target unit then moves forward until it makes contact with the target's front face. The unit cannot move through friendly or enemy units while making this move, though it may pivot through other units as long as it ends clear of them. Once it makes contact, it aligns with the target unit as normal.

Counter-Charging to the flank or rear can sometime prove slightly tricky in narrow confines. It is perfectly fine to slide the unit sideways to fit against the front of the enemy, as long as the final position does not overlap any other unit. If the unit cannot fit against the target, then it cannot Counter-Charge that unit.

All rules that apply in a Charge also apply in a Counter-Charge, unless otherwise specified.

TERRAIN

Elements of terrain make your table look more impressive, but they also make the game more complex, so don't use too much terrain in your first games of *Kings of War*. In war games, terrain is normally made in either of two ways: single terrain pieces or areas of terrain. The rules for both are below. Before the game, it's always a good idea to agree with your opponent how you are going to treat each of the pieces of terrain on the table.

Terrain Types

There are four types of terrain in *Kings of War*:

- **Blocking Terrain**

  Units cannot move across blocking terrain and must go around it. We recommend treating buildings, high walls and other large pieces as blocking terrain. The edge of the table is also normally treated as blocking terrain. Units can pivot through Blocking Terrain in the same way as other units (see Interpenetration when pivoting on page 55).

- **Difficult Terrain**

  This type of terrain consists of things like woods, crop fields, areas of rocky terrain or scree and so on. They are normally made by gluing a number of pieces of terrain onto a large base. This conveniently shows the area of the terrain – the entire area of this base counts as difficult terrain. While moving At The Double, units treat Difficult Terrain as Blocking Terrain instead.

- **Obstacles**

  Obstacles are long and narrow pieces of terrain, like a low wall, a fence, a hedge, etc. – something that a roughly man-sized creature could see over and clamber across easily. Units can move over obstacles normally (even ending their move on top of them), but cannot cross them while moving 'At the Double'. Obstacles should be no more than 1" high – any higher and they will be Blocking Terrain instead.

- **Decorative Terrain**

  Small pieces of decorative terrain, such as lone trees or bushes, are treated as decorative terrain and are ignored for all in-game purposes. Units can move over/ through them freely and can even end their move on top. It's best that decorative terrain like this is removable, but a unit's position can be marked some other way if it can't physically balance on top.

TERRAIN AND LINE OF SIGHT

Terrain Height

Heights of all terrain features should be agreed before the game. As a rough guideline, a piece of terrain has one level of height for each inch of actual physical height, so a 2" high wall would be height 2 for example. See below for some example pieces of terrain and their designations.

Obstacles are height 1 for determining cover, but never block Line of Sight.

Drawing Line of Sight

When working out Line of Sight, terrain blocks LOS to any units behind in the same way as a unit of the same height. For example, a height 2 or higher wall will block LOS between two height 2 units.

Some pieces of terrain, such as rivers and ponds, will be completely flat and never block Line of Sight. As always, these should be agreed with your opponent before the game.

Difficult Terrain

If any part of a unit is inside a piece of difficult terrain then that piece of terrain will not block LOS. In order words, areas of difficult terrain block LOS to units behind them (depending on height, of course), but not to units inside them.

Hills

While standing on a hill, a unit adds that hills height to its own. For example, a height 1 war engine on a height 2 hill would be height 3, while large infantry (height 2) would be height 4 while stood on the hill.

A unit must have the majority of its base on a hill in order to be standing on it.

SHOOT

When you're done moving all of your units, it's time to shoot with any of them that can do so. Pick one of your units at a time, choose a target for them, and let loose!

If you start the Shoot phase and have not issued orders to all of your units, it is assumed that all units you have not ordered during the Move phase have been ordered to Halt.

If a unit has two or more types of ranged attacks (including spells), it can only use one per turn.

MOVING AND SHOOTING

Units that have received an 'At the Double' order that turn are too busy moving to be able to use ranged attacks.

MELEE AND SHOOTING

Units that are in base contact with enemies cannot use or be targeted by ranged attacks, unless specifically allowed.

RANGES

The ranges of the most common weapons used in *Kings of War* are:

- Long rifles, heavy crossbows: 36"

- Bows, crossbows, rifles: 24"

- Harpoon guns, carbines, firebolts (i.e. the flaming attacks used by some supernatural creatures): 18"

- Pistols, javelins, thrown weapons: 12"

If a unit has a ranged attack with a range that is different from the ones above, it will be specified in its special rules.

Picking a Target

A unit can pick a single enemy unit as a target for its ranged attacks as long as the following conditions are met:

- the target is at least partially in the unit's arc of sight.

- the unit has line of sight to the target.

- the distance between the unit leader point and its target is equal to or less than your unit's weapon range.

SHOOTING AND HITTING THE TARGET

Once the target has been picked, roll a number of dice equal to the firing unit's Attacks value. Your unit's dice rolls, with any modifiers that apply, must score a number equal to or higher than its Ranged Attack value in order to hit its target. Discard any dice that score less than that.

Modifiers

A number of factors can affect the chance of hitting a target:

- **−1 Moving.** The firing unit received any order other than Halt that turn. This modifier does not apply to pistols, javelins, thrown weapons.

- **−1 Cover.** The target is in cover (see overleaf).

For each of these factors, deduct one from the score rolled by the dice. For example, if your unit normally needs a 4 or more to hit, but it has moved, you will need 5 or more to hit instead. If the target was in cover as well, you would need 6s.

Any dice that rolls a 1 is always a miss, regardless of modifiers. However, if modifiers to the roll mean that the unit would need more than 6 to hit, it can still use ranged attacks and will need 6 to hit, but it only rolls dice equal to half of its Attacks (rounding down).

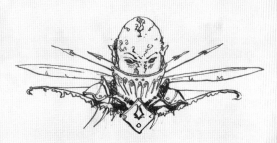

COVER

In cases when the target unit is partially visible behind a unit or terrain piece, the firing unit might suffer from the negative 'cover' modifier on its rolls to hit. To decide whether the target unit is in cover, draw LOS from the unit leader point of the firing unit to the side of the target unit that the firing unit is in (front, rear, or either flank).

A firing unit ignores any piece of terrain that it is currently within, or in base contact with, for determining whether an enemy unit is in cover, unless the enemy unit is also touching or within the same piece of terrain.

A unit which is standing on a hill ignores any intervening units or pieces of terrain that have an equal or smaller height than the hill when determining if a target is in cover, except for pieces of difficult terrain that the target is within.

The target unit will be in cover if:

- At least half of its base is within difficult terrain, or...

- LOS to at least half of the target facing is blocked, or passes over intervening units or terrain that have a smaller height than the firing or target unit.

Big Targets
Intervening units/terrain that are three height levels smaller than the target offer no cover. For example, height 1 units/terrain do not offer cover to height 4 units.

Not Sure?
In the rare, marginal cases when you're not sure whether your target is in cover or not, simply roll a die. On a 4+ it is not, on 3 or less it is.

DAMAGING THE TARGET

After discarding any dice that missed, pick up the dice and roll them again, to try and damage the enemy unit. The number your unit needs to damage the target is equal to the target's Defence value. This roll can sometimes be modified by special rules, etc.

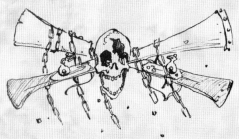

Any die that rolls a 1 always fails to damage, regardless of modifiers. If a modifier brings the score required to damage a target to above 6, that target cannot be damaged.

Recording Damage
For each hit that scores damage, place a damage marker next to the unit. This represents physical damage and casualties as well as a decline in the unit's morale, cohesion and will to fight on.

As the unit accumulates damage markers, it might be more convenient to record this by writing it down, or placing a die (possibly an unusual one, of a different size or colour, to avoid rolling it by mistake) next to a single damage marker behind the unit, or using some other suitable tokens.

TESTING NERVE

At the end of the Shoot phase, test the Nerve of any unit you inflicted damage on in that phase. This test is described on page 68, and will determine whether the damaged units stand, waver or run away.

MELEE

When you're done shooting with all of your units, it's time for your warriors to strike against the enemies that they have charged that turn. Of course, in reality the enemy warriors would be striking against yours, but for the sake of playability we imagine that in your turn the impetus of the charge means that your men will be doing most of the hacking and slashing, while the enemy mostly defend themselves. If the enemy is not annihilated or routed, your men will fall back and brace themselves, for you can be sure that the enemy will charge back into the fight during their turn to avenge their fallen comrades.

At this stage, there will be a number of combats on the table equal to the number of enemy units you charged in the Move phase. Pick one of these combats and resolve it completely before moving to the next, and so on until all combats have been resolved.

STRIKING

To attack the unit you charged, roll a number of dice equal to the charging unit's Attacks value.

If your unit is attacking an enemy to the flank, it doubles its Attacks.

If your unit is attacking an enemy to the rear, it trebles its Attacks.

HITTING THE TARGET

This process is exactly the same as described for ranged attacks, except that it

uses the unit's Melee value rather than the Ranged one, and the modifier below rather than the ones for shooting.

Modifiers

A number of factors can make a hit less likely to happen, such as a -1 modifier for Hindered charges (see below) or those from special rules.

For each of these factors, add or deduct the modifiers from the score rolled by the dice. For example, if your unit normally needs a 4 or more to hit, but is Hindered (-1 modifier), you will need 5 or more to hit instead. If you incur an additional -1 to hit, you would need 6s.

Any dice that rolls a 1 is always a miss, regardless of modifiers. However, if modifiers to the roll mean that the unit would need more than 6 to hit, it can still attack and will need 6 to hit, but it only rolls dice equal to half of its Attacks (rounding down).

Hindered Charges

If a charging unit's move has gone through or ended over any portion of difficult terrain or an obstacle then it is Hindered in the following melee phase. While Hindered, units suffer a -1 modifier when rolling to hit. A unit can only be Hindered once in any given charge, so will only ever suffer a single -1 modifier as a result of a Hindered charge.

A unit that is Counter-Charging is never Hindered, whether by terrain, special rules or any other method.

DAMAGING THE TARGET

This process is exactly the same as described for ranged attacks.

Recording Damage

This process is exactly the same as described for ranged attacks.

TESTING NERVE

At the end of each combat, if you have managed to score at least one point of Damage on the target, test the target's Nerve. This test is described on page 68, and will determine whether the damaged units stand, waver or run away.

REGROUP!

Target Destroyed – Chargers Regroup

At the end of each combat, if your unit(s) managed to rout the target, it can do one of the following:

- stay where it is and pivot around its centre to face any direction (as per a Change Facing order).

- move directly forward D6". The unit must move the full distance rolled. This move is not affected by difficult terrain and obstacles.

- move directly backwards D3" (as above).

A unit cannot move through any other units while regrouping, though it can pivot through them as long as it ends clear.

Once the Regroup move has been carried out, shuffle the unit so that there is a 1" gap between it and all enemy units, and so that it is not touching any friendly units. Move the unit the shortest distance possible in any direction to maintain the gap (usually this will be straight back 1" but use whichever direction is the shortest).

Target Remains – Chargers Pull Back

If, on the other hand, your unit did not manage to rout its enemies and is therefore still in contact with them, it must be moved directly back 1" – your warriors have been fought off and must fall back, close ranks and brace themselves for the inevitable counter-attack.

Remember at this point to separate any unit that ended up very close to other enemy units when charging the target, so that they are 1" apart once again. Also, make sure that your own units are separated by a little visible gap (a millimetre or so…).

If it is impossible to achieve the 1" distance from enemies, see if this can be done by moving said enemies away until they are 1" away. In the very rare cases when even this is impossible, then it's fine to leave them closer than 1".

DISORDERED

Units that have suffered at least one point of damage in the melee phase are Disordered – mark them with an appropriate counter.

They will remain disordered until the end of their following turn, when the Disordered counters are removed.

No Ranged Attacks

Disordered units cannot use any form of ranged attack (including magic). This is because they have been disrupted by the melee or are busy fighting back in close quarters.

NERVE

As a unit accumulates damage, it will become more and more likely to lose cohesion, until eventually it will turn tail and run from the field, never to return.

combat. In a combat where more than two units are involved, resolve all of the attacks first, and then take the Nerve test.

WHEN TO TEST

At the end of both the Move and Shoot phase of your turn, you test the Nerve of any enemy unit you managed to inflict damage upon during that phase. In the Melee phase, however, this test is done immediately at the end of each combat, if you managed to inflict damage on the target during that

HOW TO TEST

Each unit has two numbers under its Nerve value. The first number is the unit's Wavering limit, the second number is its Routing limit.

To test the Nerve of an enemy unit, roll 2D6 and add to the result the points of damage currently on the unit, plus any other

modifiers that apply (such as some special rules). This is the total you're using to 'attack' the enemy unit's Nerve. This total is then compared with the Nerve value of the enemy unit.

- If the total is equal to or higher than the unit's Routing limit, the unit suffers a Rout (see below).

- If the total is lower than the Routing limit, but equal to or higher than the Wavering limit, the unit suffers from a Wavering result (see below).

- If the total is lower than the unit's Wavering limit, then the unit is said to be Steady, which means it is completely unaffected and continues to fight on as normal.

For example, let's assume you are testing the Nerve of an enemy unit that has a Nerve of 11/13 and has suffered 3 points of damage. If you roll a seven or less, your total will be ten or less and the enemy will be Steady. If you roll an eight or nine, your total will be eleven or twelve and the enemy will be Wavering. If you roll a ten or more, the enemy Routs!

Steady

The unit continues to fight normally and does not suffer any negative effects. Remember however that units capable of ranged attacks, which have been Disordered will not be able to use their ranged attacks in their next turn.

Wavering

The unit does not rout, but is severely shaken during its next turn. In its next Move phase, it can only be given one of the following orders: Halt, Change Facing or Back. In addition, the unit is Disordered (so it will not be able to use its ranged attacks in its next Shoot phase).

It is normally a good idea to mark Wavering units with a token of some kind (like a bit of cotton wool).

Rout!

The unit routs of the field, is butchered to a man, or surrenders to the enemy and is taken prisoner – in any case, as far as this game is concerned, it is destroyed. Remove it.

EXCEPTIONAL MORALE RESULTS

Double Six – We Are Doomed!

If you roll double six when testing Nerve and the unit is not Routed, it will still suffer from a result of Wavering, as insidious news of defeat start to spread through the ranks.

Double One – Hold Your Ground!

If you roll snake eyes (double one) when testing Nerve, the enemy is filled with implacable resolve and will always be Steady and fight on, regardless of any modifier.

FEARLESS!

A few units in the game have a value of "-" for their Wavering Limit. For example, they could be -/14. These units are normally composed of fanatical, frenzied warriors or mindless supernatural creatures - in any case, they cannot Waver, and will therefore remain Steady until they eventually Rout.

Of course a routing result for such troops represents them being utterly annihilated, or collpasing as their magical lifeforce abandons them.

WAR ENGINES

Following are all of the exceptions that apply to War Engine units, unless differently specified in their entry.

Move

War Engines cannot be ordered to move At the Double, nor to Charge. While moving, War Engines treat obstacles as blocking terrain.

Melee

Attacking War Engines

Units attacking a War Engine always treble their Attacks, regardless of position.

Remember also that even if it survived such an onslaught, a War Engine would become Disordered as normal.

Shooting

Unless otherwise specified, War Engines have a range of 48".

Arc of Sight

If a War Engine's base is wider than 50mm, then its arc of sight is not taken from the corners. Instead the 50mm wide arc should be defined on the unit's base, such as by painting two vertical lines on the front or marking it with appropriate scenic decoration. It still has a front arc as normal, but when choosing a target for ranged attacks it may only choose one within the arc of sight taken from the 50mm marked on the base.

For example, the base shown right has an 80mm width, but the arc of sight only extends from a 50mm width on the front of the base.

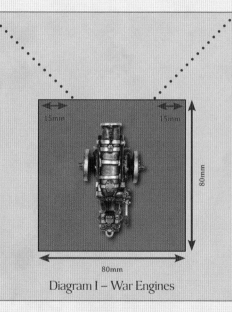

Diagram I – War Engines

INDIVIDUALS

Units with this rule are normally made of a single model representing a roughly man-sized individual, on foot or horseback. These obviously behave in a very different manner from regimented units or very large creatures. The following rules represent this:

Line of Sight

Before being given an order, an individual may pivot to face any direction for free.

Individuals never block line of sight or offer cover against ranged attacks.

Move

Individuals have the Nimble special rule.

Shooting

Individuals may pivot to face any direction for free before picking a target in the shooting phase.

Enemies shooting against Individuals suffer an additional -1 to hit modifier.

Melee

When charging an individual, a unit must make contact with the face that they started in as normal, however the Individual will turn to align flush with the unit's facing, rather than the unit aligning to the individual's facing.

Enemies never double/treble their Attacks when fighting the individual (including against Individual War Engines).

Similarly, the individual does not double/treble its own attacks when attacking an enemy in the flank/rear. It does still treble its attacks against war engines, however.

If an individual is routed and the charger (including another individual) decides to advance D6" directly forward, it can make contact with another enemy unit. This is treated as a successful charge and the charger is lined up against the new enemy as normal and can immediately attack again!

If either the initial charge move or the regroup move took the charging unit over an obstacle or through difficult terrain, then it is hindered during this additional combat.

Also note that if the new enemy is another individual, which is then routed, the charger can again advance D6" forward as above, and so on – you can run over any number of meddling individuals in a single charge!

SPECIAL RULES

Some units, or even entire armies, possess what we call 'special rules'. Each of these special rules is an exception to the normal rules. Some are listed with the units themselves, but the most common are listed below.

Big Shield

If you are worried about not finding any cover, best bring it with you to the battle!

All attacks (ranged and melee) from enemies that are in the unit's front arc treat its defence as 6+.

Blast (n)

This rule is used for all weapons that explode on impact with the target or otherwise inflict massive amounts of damage with a single hit.

If the unit's attack hits the target, the target suffers a number of hits equal to the number in brackets, rather than a single hit.

For example, if a unit suffers a hit from a *Blast (D6+3)* attack, it will suffer from four to nine hits rather than a single one. Once this is done, roll for damage as normal for all of the hits caused.

Breath Attack (n)

This rule is used for dragon breath and other attacks where a great gout of flame or toxic gas fills an area.

The unit has a ranged attack for which you roll (n) dice rather than the Attacks value of the unit. This attack has a range of 12" and always hits on 4+, regardless of any modifier.

Sometimes this rule is listed as Breath Attack (Att). In this case use the unit's Attacks stat as the value for n.

Brutal

To be showered with the life fluids and innards of one's former comrades is a rather unnerving experience...

When testing the Nerve of an enemy unit in melee with one or more of your units with this rule, add +1 to the total.

Crushing Strength (n)

This rule is used to represent the devastating effects of melee hits from creatures of terrible strength or that are equipped with very heavy close combat weapons or even magical weaponry.

All melee hits inflicted by the unit have a +(n) modifier when rolling to damage.

Elite

Creatures with this rule are supremely skilled – true masters of the art of war.

Whenever the unit rolls to hit, it can re-roll all dice that score a natural, unmodified 1.

Ensnare

This rule is used to represent all of the means, both physiscal and supernatural, to slow down an enemy's momentum – from weighted nets to beguiling spells.

When attacking this unit in its front, enemies suffer an additional -1 to hit in melee.

Fly

This rule can literally represent flying movement (not really soaring high in the sky, however... more like fluttering around, a bit like a chicken), or even a ghostly creature's ability to move through solid matter.

The unit can move over anything (blocking terrain, enemy units, friendly units when charging, etc.), but still cannot land on top of them. The unit does not suffer hindered charges for moving over difficult terrain or obstacles, unless it ends the move within or touching them. The unit also has the *Nimble* special rule.

Fury

Some warriors and creatures are just too frenzied with bloodlust to ever slow down in their relentless assault.

While wavered, this unit may declare a Counter-Charge.

Headstrong

"Wavering's for little wide-eyed girls with ribbons in their hair... and Elves." – Dwarf proverb.

Whenever the unit begins a turn Wavering, it rolls a die. On a 4+ it shrugs off the effects of Wavering and is Disordered instead.

Indirect Fire

The unit fires its shots in high arcing trajectories, which means that the distance to the target is pretty much irrelevant and that most cover is pretty much useless. However, if any enemies get really close, it's impossible to hit them.

The unit fires in high arcs, hitting the target from the top, which means it does not suffers the –1 to hit modifier for cover.

On the other hand, the unit cannnot shoot targets that are within 12".

Note that the firing unit does still need to see its target to fire at it.

Individual

This rule is explained on page 71.

Inspiring

The bravery of a heroic general, or the presence of a great big flag, can convince warriors to stand their ground a little longer. For creatures like the undead (that don't care much about banners), the proximity of their general or of a sorcerous banner fills them with supernatural energy.

If this unit, or any friendly non-allied unit within 6" of this unit, is Routed, the opponent must re-roll that Nerve test. The second result stands.

Note a unit can also have Inspiring (specific unit) – in that case the unit will only inspire itself and that unit.

Iron Resolve

Some elite troops can hold their ground even when they have taken horrendous casualties.

If this unit is Steady as a result of a nerve test, it regains 1 point of damage previously suffered.

Lifeleech(n)

The blood and life energy of the enemy are sustainance for these unnatural creatures.

In a melee, this unit regains one point of damage it has previously suffered for every point of damage it deals, up to a maximum of n.

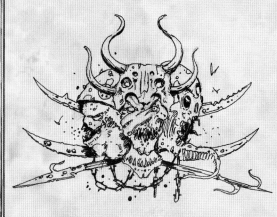

Nimble

Used for flyers, lightly armed units like skirmishers and scouting cavalry, and heroic individuals that venture on the battlefield on their own, this rule makes the unit considerably more manoeuvrable and more suited at using their ranged weapons to harass the enemy.

The unit can make a single extra pivot of up to 90 degrees around its centre while executing any move order, including a Charge! It cannot make this extra pivot when ordered to Halt.

In addition, the unit does not suffer from the −1 to hit modifier for moving and shooting.

Pathfinder

Mystical affinity to nature or simply a very good eye for terrain?

The unit suffers no movement penalties for difficult terrain, simply treating it as open terrain.

Pathfinder units are not Hindered for charging through difficult terrain.

Phalanx

From the front, these units look like a forest of sharp spikes pointing at you.

Units that charge this unit's front cannot use the Thunderous Charge special rule.

Piercing(n)

This rule is used for ranged attacks that can penetrate armour with ease (such as shots from rifles), as well as magical ranged attacks.

All ranged hits inflicted by the unit have a +(n) modifier when rolling to damage.

Regeneration (n)

Creatures gifted with this ability are very difficult to kill, as their wounds heal at incredible speed.

Every time this unit receives a move order (including Halt!), before doing anything else, roll a number of dice equal to the amount of damage currently on the unit. For every result of (n) or higher, the unit recovers a point of damage.

Reload!

Some powerful missile weapons take much longer to reload, making them less flexible.

The unit can fire only if it received a Halt order that turn.

Shambling

Braiiinsss... braiiiinnnssss...

The unit cannot be ordered 'At the Double', except when carrying out a Vanguard move.

Stealthy

The unit is extremely adept at hiding or benefits from magical protection that makes it very difficult to target with ranged attacks.

Enemies shooting against the unit suffer an additional -1 to hit modifier.

Strider

The unit is big enough or agile enough to brush past any barrier.

The unit never suffers the penalty for Hindered charges.

Thunderous Charge (n)

This rule is used for mounted knights equipped with lances and other units that rely on momentum to deliver a powerful charge.

All melee hits inflicted by the unit have a +(n) modifier when rolling to damage. This bonus is in addition to the unit's Crushing Strength (if any), however the unit loses this bonus when Disordered or during Hindered charges.

Vanguard

This unit is trained to range ahead of the main force, scouting the terrain and gathering information about the enemy.

The unit can make a single At the Double or Advance order after set-up is finished. If both armies have units with this rule, roll a die. The highest scorer decides who begins to move one of their *Vanguard* units first, then the players alternate until all *Vanguard* units have been moved.

Very Inspiring

The best leaders are able to command every unit on the battlefield by use of sorcery or numerous brave messengers.

This is the same as the *Inspiring* special rule, except that it has a range of 9". Any rule which affects *Inspiring* also affects *Very Inspiring*.

Vicious

The unit fights with utter ferocity, resorting to serrated blades and wicked hooks, eye gouging and all manner of other unsporting behaviour.

Whenever the unit rolls to damage, it can re-roll all dice that score a natural, unmodified 1.

Yellow Bellied

What did the boss-man say? It sounded like 'retreat'... yes, I'm pretty sure it was that...

When this unit wishes to charge an enemy unit's front facing, roll a die. If the result is a 1 then the unit 'misunderstands' the order and carries out a Halt! order instead.

This does not apply if the unit wishes to charge the flank or rear of an enemy unit, an individual or war engine, or if it is carrying out a Counter-Charge.

Picking a Force

You can play *Kings of War* with just a few units per side, without worrying about the two sides being equally matched. This is great for learning the game, but after you've become familiar with the rules and have amassed a large collection of models, you might want to try a game where the forces facing one another across the battlefield are balanced, so that both players have an equal chance of winning the game.

In order to achieve this, you and your opponent must pick an army before the game. First agree a total of points, say for example 2,000 points. Then start picking units from one of the force lists provided in this book – each unit costs a certain amount of points, as listed in its entry in the appropriate force list (including any options like magical artefacts). For example a regiment will cost around 100 points.

As you pick them and include them in your army, keep adding their cost until you have reached the total you agreed. You can of course spend less than the agreed total, but you cannot spend even a single point more. However, an army is still considered to be the size of the maximum total the players agreed on (e.g. an army which come to 1995 points would still be considered a 2000 point army).

Army Selection

In order to restrict the possible (nasty) combinations that can be fielded and to make sure armies have a resemblance of 'realism' about them, we introduce the following limitations to the unit types that can make up your army:

Troops

Your army can include up to 2 Troops per Regiment in the army.

Your army can also include up to 4 Troops per Horde in the army.

Regiments

Your army can include as many Regiments as you like. For every Regiment in the army, you can also include the following:

   1 War Engine OR 1 Monster OR 1 Hero

For example, including 3 Regiments gives you access to up to 3 additional units chosen from War Engines, Heroes or Monsters.

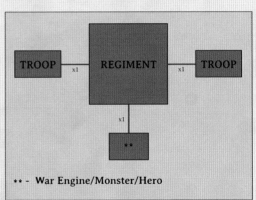

** – War Engine/Monster/Hero

Hordes

Your army can include as many Hordes as you like.

For every Horde in the army, you can also include the following:

   Up to 1 war engine and 1 hero and
   1 monster.

For example, including 3 Hordes gives you access to up to 3 additional War Engines, up to 3 additional Heroes AND up to 3 additional Monsters.

Legions

Legions are Hordes for the purposes of army selection.

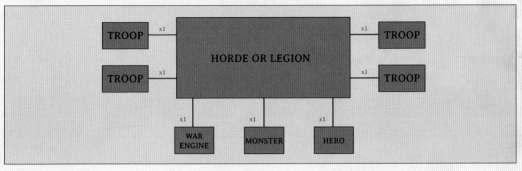

Irregular Units

Note that some units have an asterisk next to their name (for example: Gargoyles*). We call these *irregular units*, because they are not representative of the core, or mainstay force, of their army. This means that the unit is treated as a Troop from the point of view of Army Selection, even if it is a Regiment or Horde – i.e. it does not unlock any optional Troops, Heroes, Monsters or War Engines, and it needs to be unlocked by a Regiment, Horde or Legion of 'regular' troops.

Heroes (Monsters)

Heroes that belong to the Monster unit type (Hero (Mon)) simply count as a Hero from the point of view of force selection. So if you have a Horde, you can field a Hero (Mon) as well as a Monster.

Living Legends

In addition, if a unit has [1] after its name in the list, it is a Living Legend and this means that only one such unit exists and can therefore be included in an army. Of course it might happen that both opponents field this unit... in which case one of them must surely be an impostor and only the test of battle can show which one!

ALLIES & ALIGNMENTS

When using allies, you are free to mix units from different army lists in your army, as long as you always keep in mind that you need Regiment/Hordes of a specific army to include Troops, War Engines, Heroes or Monsters of that race, as normal.

Smaller Games

If you are a new player with a small model collection you sometimes want to throw a few units on the table to learn the game. You might even be running a small demo of the game for friends or even teaching the kids the joys of war-gaming. Whatever the circumstances, you might want to consider allowing any number of Troops in an army when playing games below around 750 points. This allows both sides to field a decent variety on unit types and for players who are still collecting their armies to get them on the table and play some games.

If you are using allies then you may only choose up to 25% of your points limit from the allied list. You may not take Living Legends as Allies. In addition, alliances between races that are hated enemies in the *Kings of War* background are not very 'realistic', so we have given a specific Alignment to each army – either Good, Evil or Neutral.

Good races should never ally with Evil races, but anybody can ally with Neutral races. So please don't mix Evil and Good units in the same army, unless your opponent agrees, of course. You can also join forces with your friends and play with several allied armies on either or both sides, as long as the points values are balanced.

MAGICAL ARTEFACTS

Magical artefacts bestow bonuses to the unit they are given to. Each unit can have a single artefact chosen from the list below, which is normally carried by the unit's Leader. The cost of the artefact is added to that of the unit.

Unless the artefact specifies otherwise, the following limits also apply:

- Each artefact is unique and therefore can only be chosen once per army.

- War Engine units cannot choose artefacts.

- Monster units cannot choose artefacts. But Hero (Mon) units definitely can.

- Living Legends (i.e. units with a [1] limit) cannot choose artefacts.

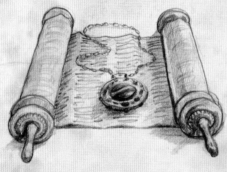

Artefacts are magical in nature (some of them might even be sentient!), and all of them have the magical power of changing their shape. This allows them to morph into a weapon, piece of armour, jewel or other implement that is more akin to the race of the warrior carrying it. For example, a Blade of Slashing could be an elegant sword in the hands of an Elf, but will turn into a crude meat cleaver in the hands of an Orc. This magical property is of course very convenient from the point of view of the average war gamer!

As the presence of these items is not obvious, players must tell their opponent which artefact any of their units is carrying

as they deploy them on the battlefield. If both players agree before deployment, you may want to play with 'hidden artefacts'. This is somewhat less fair, but can be considerably more fun...

When an item refers to 'normal' ranged attacks, it cannot be used with Breath Attack or Spells.

Blade of Slashing   Cost: 5 pts

Whenever the unit rolls to hit in Melee, it can re-roll one of the dice that failed to hit.

Fire-Oil   Cost: 5 pts

Against units with the Regeneration rule this unit gains an additional Piercing (1) on 'normal' ranged attacks, and Crushing Strength (1) in melee.

Kevinar's Flying Hammer   Cost: 5 pts

The unit has a ranged attack for which you roll a single die, regardless of the Attacks value of the unit. This attack has a range of 12" and always hits on 4+, regardless of modifiers, and if a hit is scored, it is resolved at Piercing (2).

Mace of Crushing   Cost: 5 pts

Whenever the unit rolls to damage in melee, it can re-roll one of the dice that failed to damage.

War-bow of Kaba   Cost: 5 pts

The unit has a ranged attack for which you roll a single die, regardless of the Attacks value of the unit. This attack has a range of 24" and, when rolling to hit, the unit uses a basic Ra value of 4+, regardless of its actual Ra value. The roll to hit is affected as normal by to-hit modifiers, and if a hit is scored, it is resolved at Piercing (1).

Dwarven Ale
Cost: 10 pts

The unit has the Headstrong special rule.

Myrddin's Amulet of the Fire-heart
Cost: 10 pts

Once per game, after using a ranged attack or spell, this unit may immediately use another different ranged attack or spell it possesses, against the same or a different target.

Piercing Arrow
Cost: 10 pts

Whenever the unit rolls to damage with a 'normal' ranged attack, it can re-roll one of the dice that failed to damage.

Quicksilver Rapier
Cost: 10 pts

This unit has +1 to hit when attacking individuals in melee.

Brew of Courage
Cost: 15 pts

When testing Nerve against this unit, the enemies suffer an additional -1 to their total.

Brew of Haste
Cost: 15 pts

The unit has +1 Speed.

Pipes of Terror
Cost: 15 pts

The unit has the Brutal special rule.

Blade of the Beast Slayer
Cost: 20 pts

This artefact can only be used by Heroes.

The Hero has Crushing Strength (2) when attacking large infantry, large cavalry, monsters or heroes who do not have the Individual special rule. If the Hero already has Crushing Strength, it is increased by 2 when attacking those same targets.

Darklord's Onyx Ring
Cost: 20 pts

This artefact can only be used by Heroes with the Regeneration rule. The unit's Regeneration value is increased by 1. For example, a unit with Regeneration (5+) now has Regeneration (4+).

Helm of Confidence   Cost: 20 pts

You must always re-roll a rout result for this unit even if they are not in range of a unit with inspiring.

Inspiring Talisman   Cost: 20 pts

This artefact can only be used by Heroes. The Hero has the Inspiring special rule.

Maccwar's Potion of the Caterpillar   Cost: 20 pts

The unit has the Pathfinder special rule.

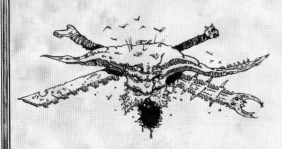

Blessing of the Gods   Cost: 25 pts

The unit has the Elite special rule.

Chant of Hate   Cost: 25 pts

The unit has the Vicious special rule.

Kaba's Holy Hand Grenades   Cost: 25 pts

The unit has a ranged attack for which you roll a single die, regardless of the Attacks value of the unit.

This attack has a range of 12" and always hits on 4+, regardless of modifiers. The attack also has the Blast (D6) and Piercing (2) special rule.

Scarletmaw's Fenulian Amulet   Cost: 25 pts

Units with the Lightning Bolt spell only. This item increases the unit's Lightning Bolt (n) value by 2. For example, Lightning Bolt (3) becomes Lightning Bolt (5).

Boots of Levitation   Cost: 30 pts

This artefact can only be used by Heroes. The Hero can Advance and then shoot as if it had Halted that turn. It can also move At the Double and shoot as if it had Advanced that turn.

Brew of Strength   Cost: 30 pts

The unit has Crushing Strength (1), or if the unit already has Crushing Strength, it is increased by 1.

Crepognon's Scrying Gem of Zellak   Cost: 30 pts

When starting to deploy their units, your opponent must deploy D3+1 units instead of a single one.

Diadem of Dragon-kind   Cost: 30 pts

The unit has the Breath Attack (10) rule.

Healing Charm   Cost: 30 pts

This artefact can only be used by Heroes. The Hero has the Heal (3) spell.

Heart-seeking Chant   Cost: 30 pts

The unit's ranged attacks and spells have the Piercing (1) special rule, or if the unit already has Piercing, it is increased by 1.

Mreb's Grimoire of Unspeakable Darkness   Cost: 30 pts

Units with the Surge special rule only. This item increases the unit's Surge (n) value by 4. For example, Surge (8) becomes Surge (12).

The Boomstick   Cost: 30 pts

This artefact can only be used by Heroes. The Hero has the Lightning Bolt (3) spell.

Boots of the Seven Leagues   Cost: 35 pts

This artefact can only be used by a Hero with the Individual special rule. The Hero has the Vanguard special rule.

Ensorcelled Armour Cost: 35 pts

This artefact can only be used by Heroes. The Hero's Defence is improved by 1, to a maximum of 6+.

Jar of the Four Winds Cost: 35 pts

The unit's 'normal' ranged attacks gain 12" to their range.

Medallion of Life Cost: 35 pts

This artefact can only be used by Heroes. The Hero has the Regeneration(5+) special rule.

Orcsbain's Amulet of Thorns Cost: 35 pts

The unit has the Phalanx special rule.

The Fog Cost: 35 pts

The unit has the Stealthy special rule.

Wine of Elvenkind Cost: 40 pts

The unit has the Nimble special rule.

Wings of Honeymaze Cost: 40 pts

This artefact can only be used by a Hero with the Individual rule. The Hero has the Fly special rule and increases their speed to 10.

Brew of Keen-eyeness Cost: 45 pts

The unit has +1 to hit with 'normal' ranged attacks.

Brew of Sharpness Cost: 45 pts

The unit has +1 to hit in melee.

Crystal Pendant of Retribution Cost: 50 pts

When the unit is Routed, all units in base contact with it suffer 2D6 hits at Piercing (3). These hits are resolved by the player that Routed the unit with the Crystal, which now has to (grudgingly, we're sure) resolve the hits against their own unit(s). After the damage has been resolved, no Nerve test is taken by the damaged units – they proceed to Regroup, but cannot move directly forward D6" for their Regroup action, deterred by the huge explosion.

SPELLS

The spells listed below summarize in brief the wealth of subtly different magical powers wielded by the spellcasters of the world of Mantica, which we refer to with the generic term of 'Wizards'. A wizard is any unit that has access to the spells below, and not a unit that is equipped with a magical artefact that reproduces the effects of a spell (like the Boomstick, for example).

Spells are ranged attacks and thus follow the normal rules for shooting (e.g. a model that moves at the Double cannot use these powers that turn), with the exceptions listed below.

For spells, you always roll the number of dice indicated in the (n) value in the Wizard's entry for that spell, rather than the Att value of the Wizard itself. The Att value of the Wizard is only used if the model was to use a normal ranged attack, like a bow, instead of its spells.

Spells always hit on 4+ and ignore all to-hit modifiers for ranged attacks, including any modifiers from special rules. Note that re-rolls (like the one provided by the Elite rule), unlike modifiers, do apply.

Some spells can only target a friendly unit – this is marked as 'friendly unit only'. Note that such spells cannot normally target the wizard itself and cannot target friendly allied units – so a wizard from your main force can't bane chant an allied unit for example, and a wizard from your allied force can't heal a unit from your main force.

Each wizard's individual entry lists which spells can be purchased for him/her, much in the same way as equipment, and how much each additional spell is going to cost. This allows you to customise your wizards for your favourite battlefield role. Keep in mind, however, that a unit can make only a single shooting attack per turn, so buying more than one spell gives your wizard flexibility, as you can choose which one to use, but does not allow the Wizard to cast more than one spell per turn.

Spell	Range	Special Rules
Fireball (n)	12"	None – roll to damage as normal.
Bane-chant (n)	12"	Friendly unit only, including units engaged in combat. Hits don't inflict damage. Instead, if one or more hits are scored, for the rest of the turn all of the unit's melee and ranged attacks increase their Piercing and Crushing Strength value by 1, or gain Piercing (1) and Crushing Strength (1) if they don't already have these rules. Note that multiple bane-chants hitting the same unit do not have cumulative effects.
Wind Blast (n)	18"	Hits don't inflict damage. Instead, each hit pushes the target enemy unit 1" directly backwards if the caster is in the target unit's front arc, directly sideways and away from the caster if the caster is in either of the target unit's flank arcs, or directly forwards if the caster is in the target unit's rear arc. The target stops 1" away from enemy units or just out of contact with blocking terrain and friends. This spell has no effect on units with a speed of 0.
Lightning Bolt (n)	24"	Piercing (1) – roll to damage as normal.
Heal (n)	12"	Friendly unit only, including units engaged in combat. Hits don't inflict damage. Instead, for every hit 'inflicted', the friendly unit removes a point of damage that it has previously suffered.
Surge (n)	12"	Friendly unit with the Shambling special rule only. Hits don't inflict damage. Instead, for every hit 'inflicted', the Shambling friendly unit moves straight forward a full inch (stopping just out of contact from friendly units and blocking terrain). If this movement brings it into contact with an enemy unit, treat this as a successful charge against the enemy facing that has been contacted. However, the charged unit will not take any Nerve tests for any damage it might have taken previously in that Shoot phase. If the Surge move took the unit over an obstacle or through difficult terrain then it will be hindered in the ensuing combat as normal. This spell has no effect on units with a speed of 0.

GAME SCENARIOS

1) Prepare your Forces

First of all you and your opponent need to pick armies to an agreed total of points, using the process described in 'Picking a Force', on page 76.

2) Choose a Gaming Area

We assume that games of *Kings of War* will be played on a 6'x4' foot table or other flat surface, like a floor.

For larger games, we recommend an extra 3' of width for every 1000 points over 2000. For games with 1500 or fewer points, we recommend using a smaller board size, like 4'x4'.

3) Determine Scenario

So, how do you win the game? Each scenario has a different set of objectives to complete, as described below. To determine which scenario you and your opponent will play, roll a die:

D6	Type of Game
1	Kill!
2	Invade!
3	Dominate!
4	Pillage!
5	Loot!
6	Kill and Pillage!

4) Place Terrain

Before the game, it's a good idea if you and your opponent put some terrain on the battlefield. Arrange it in a sensible manner, trying to recreate a plausible landscape of the fantastic world your armies are battling in. Alternatively, find a third and neutral person to lay out the terrain for you.

During this stage it's vital that you agree what each piece of terrain is going to count as during the game –is it blocking terrain, an obstacle, a piece of decorative terrain or an area of difficult terrain?

5) Set-up

After rolling for the type of game and setting up the objectives/loot, if any, both players roll a die. The person scoring highest chooses one long edge of the battlefield as their own and then places one of their units on that side of the battlefield, more than 12" from the middle line (see Set-Up diagram). Their opponent then does the same on the opposite side of the table. The players keep alternating in doing this until they have placed all of their units onto the table.

6) Who Goes First?

Both you and your opponent roll a die. The highest scorer chooses whether they are going to have the first turn or give the first turn to their opponent instead. Game on!

7) Duration

The game lasts until each player has taken six turns. At the end of turn 6, one player rolls a die. On a 1-3 the game ends. On a 4-6 both players play an extra turn and then the game ends – work out the winner as described in the scenario conditions.

You can of course vary the number of turns you want to play for, or decide to play for a set amount of time instead (e.g. two hours), after which the game continues until each player has had the same number of turns. Alternatively, you could also play a Timed Game, as explained in the Timed Games section (page 88).

SCENARIO 1: KILL!

Objective

At the end of the game, add up the cost of all of enemy units you Routed. That is your score. Your opponent does the same and you compare scores.

If the difference between the scores in favour of a player is at least 10% of the total cost of the armies, that player wins, otherwise the game is a draw. For example, in a game where armies are 2,000 points, you need at least 200 points more than your opponent to win.

SCENARIO 2: INVADE!

Objective

At the end of the game, add up the cost of all of your units that are entirely inside the opponent's half of the table. That is your score. Your opponent does the same and you compare scores.

If the difference between the scores in favour of a player is at least 10% of the total cost of the armies, that player wins, otherwise the game is a draw. For example, in a game where armies are 2,000 points, you need at least 200 points more than your opponent to win.

SCENARIO 3: DOMINATE!

Objective

At the end of the game, add up the cost of all of your units that are entirely within 12" of the centre of the playing area. That is your score. Your opponent does the same and you compare scores.

If the difference between the scores in favour of a player is at least 10% of the total cost of the armies, that player wins, otherwise the game is a draw. For example, in a game where armies are 2,000 points, you need at least 200 points more than your opponent to win.

Set-Up Diagram

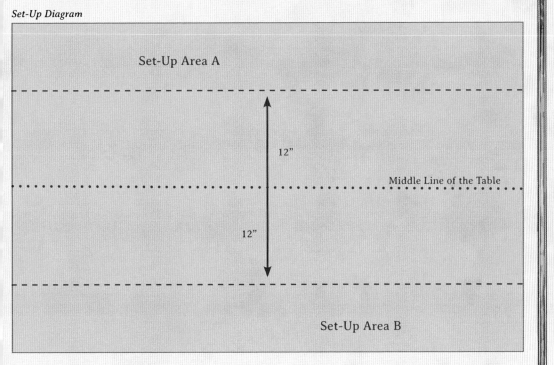

Set-Up Area A

12"

Middle Line of the Table

12"

Set-Up Area B

SCENARIO 4: PILLAGE!

Set-up

Place D3+4 objective markers on the battlefield before rolling for set-up. For objective markers you should use 25 mm round bases, but two pence coins or other items of similar size are also acceptable. Objective markers cannot be placed within Blocking Terrain.

Both players roll a die. Whoever scores highest places a marker anywhere on the battlefield. Players then take turns to place objective markers, which must be more than 12" apart from one another.

Objective

If, at the end of the game you have at least a unit within 3" of an objective and there are no enemy units within 3" of it, you control that objective. A single unit can control any number of objectives.

If you control more objectives than your opponent, you win, otherwise the game is a draw.

Individuals are always ignored from the point of view of controlling objectives (if it helps, remove them from the table before determining control of objectives).

SCENARIO 5: LOOT!

Set-up

Before rolling for set up, place 3 loot markers on the battlefield (same size as objective markers); one in the dead centre of battlefield, and then the players each place one other loot marker on the centre line at least 12" away from other loot markers. Players dice off to determine who places their loot marker first. Loot Counters cannot be placed in Blocking Terrain.

Controlling Loot Markers

During the game, when one of your units **ends** its ends its move (excluding Vanguard moves) over a loot counter, it can pick it up. That unit will then carry the loot counter.

While carrying a loot counter, a unit's speed is reduced to 5 (unless it is already

less than 5) and it cannot be targeted by Wind Blast or Surge.

A unit can drop any loot counters it is carrying at the start of any move - simply place the counter(s) anywhere in base contact with the unit and then move the unit as normal.

Units with one or more loot counters can leave the battle by moving into contact with their own table edge. If your unit leaves the battle it cannot return, but the loot counters it is carrying are safe.

If one of your units is Routed while carrying loot, place the counters anywhere within its footprint before removing the unit. If the unit was destroyed in a melee, your opponent automatically distributes the loot counters however they like among the units that are in contact with yours before your unit is removed.

Individuals cannot pick up nor carry the Loot – the best they can do is stand on a loot counter to defend it – as long as an individual is standing on a Loot counter, it cannot be picked up by the enemy.

Objective

At the end of the game you score one point for each loot counter in possession of one of your units, including those that have left the battle. If you score more points than your opponent, you win, otherwise the game is a draw.

SCENARIO 6: KILL AND PILLAGE!

Set-up

Follow the same process described for scenario 4: Pillage!

Objective

At the end of the game count the points just like in a Kill game. In addition to points for Routing units, however, any objective you control at the end of the game (as described in Pillage) is worth an amount of points equal to 10% of the total cost of the armies. For example, in a game where armies are 2,000 points, each objective is worth 200 points.

TIMED GAMES

We really enjoy playing *Kings of War* in a relaxed atmosphere, accompanied by epic music, beer, pizza and the unavoidable truculent banter. However, the game is designed so that you can also decide to introduce another dimension to the fight: time. This way you'll be able to experience some of the pressure of real battle, when snap decisions make the difference between victory or defeat, life or death!

Chess Clocks

The best tool for timed games is a chess clock, a device that ensures time is equally divided amongst the players, thus creating the ultimate fair and balanced war game.

Simply agree a number of turns for the game and an amount of time per player, and set the chess clock accordingly. For a 2,000 points game, we suggest six turns each and forty-five minutes per player, but it's up you to find the pace you prefer for your games.

After deciding which player begins to set-up, start that player's clock. Once that player has set up their first unit, stop their clock, start their opponent's clock and so on. Once set-up is finished, stop both clocks and roll to see who has the first turn. Once the winner of the roll has made their choice, re-start that player's clock. That player plays a turn then stops their clock and activates the opponent's clock, and so on.

The game ends at the agreed number of turns and victory conditions are worked out as normal. However, if you happen to run out of time during one of your turns, the game ends instantly and your entire army routs – immediately remove all of your remaining units, as if they suffered a Rout result, and work out the victory conditions as normal. However, in an objective-based game (like 'Pillage' or 'Kill and Pillage', in the Scenarios section), your opponent is allowed to keep moving their units for as many turns as there are left in the game in order to grab objectives before the victory conditions are worked out.

Other Timers

If you don't have a chess clock at hand, don't worry – the stopwatch in your phone or watch, or even an hourglass or egg timer will do fine. If you use one of these, then each player gets an agreed amount of time per turn (agree first how many turns the game is going to last for). We suggest that each turn should take around two minutes per 500 points in your game (say 8 minutes in a 2,000 points game). If you run out of time during your turn, your move ends and any melee that has not been fought yet is cancelled – move the chargers back 1".

Make sure you set a time limit for set-up (30 seconds per unit works fine).

Be Nice!

Of course it's only fair to stop the chess clock or timer if one of the players is distracted from the game (by a phone call or the like), or if the players need to check a rule, an unclear line of sight, etc. It is also best if any unit you destroy during your turn is removed by the opponent, together with all of its damage markers, at the beginning of their turn.

By all means, you and your opponent can vary the amount of time you have for your game or your turns according to your own taste, but if you're like us, you are going to love the pressure created by timed games – after all, in real war one rarely has the luxury of time...

FORCE LISTS

FORCES OF BASILEA

At its height, the ancient human republic of Primovantor was one of the greatest civilisations in the world, rivalling Elvenhome and the mightiest Dwarf Holds in size, power and opulence. The Celestians themselves were friends to the learned scholars of Primovantor, and humanity's power was at its very apex.

Primovantor, like much of the world, vanished under the sea at the end of the war with Winter. By that point, the God War had ravaged much of its lands, the splitting of the Celestians hitting the republic harder than any other place. Some say that it was a mercy of sorts when Primovantor sank beneath the waves of the Great Flood, wiping clean the bloated and fragmented place that it had become.

Forces of Basilea Special Rules

Alignment: Good

Blessed Be The Pious
All units in this list have the Iron Resolve special rule, unless specified otherwise.

The twin cities of Primovantor and the Golden Horn, perched atop their mountainous bedrocks, were spared the scouring of Winter's floods. Primovantor by that point had already fallen, becoming a desolate wasteland in the wake of the God War, and it stands to this day as a monument to the follies of that long forgotten age. The Golden Horn became the centre of humanity's rebirth in the years following the Great Flood, its succession of rulers struggling to bind their people together in the face of threats from every direction.

The belligerent dwarfs had retreated underground, determined no longer to involve themselves in affairs outside their own. The elves fragmented along the lines of the shattered remains of their former glories, concerned more with their own survival than the matters of lesser races. In the face of this abandonment, men faced creatures of the Abyss, marauding orcs and goblins, and even the savage men of the steppes, alone. Humanity teetered on the brink of extinction many times over those dark centuries, surviving by dint of sheer tenacity. Even the Shining Ones, the broken remains of their former patrons the Celestians, had become unreliable and fickle.

It was at the last, when all hope seemed lost, when the Hegemon Bolisean's armies were exhausted, surrounded and cut off by a far larger orc horde, that the balance

shifted. Bolisean was alone, his guards smashed into the mud, a fresh charge of orcs pounding towards him, and his blade shattered. Slumping to his knees, Bolisean threw his head back and bellowed a plea to the lightning-streaked skies above for the Shining Ones to descend and save him and his people. In return, he offered the eternal and heartfelt fealty of him and his people to the Shining Ones as the true gods of humanity.

Whether his plea caught the fickle Shining Ones in a favourable mood by chance, or whether there was something different in his cries that moved them, none will ever know. But what happened next passed forever into legend.

The spirit of Domivar himself – the son of Mescator and the hero who smote the wicked ones into the Abyss at the end of the God War, appeared before Bolisean, and asked him to repeat his oath, sealing it with his own blood in the sacred ground on which he knelt. Without thinking to

pause, Bolisean sliced open his palm on the jagged end of his sword, allowing several drops to mix with the wet filth of the ground. The reaction was instant. The rains stopped with a thundercrack of pressure and a blinding flash of lightning. As the eyes of all present adjusted in the aftermath, it was to the sight of thousands of Elohi, the winged warrior guardians of the Shining Ones, standing ready over the men of the Golden Horn. The orcs faltered, and were destroyed. The magnificent and terrible creatures overwhelmed them with violence and fury that even their savage nature could not match. The pact had been made in blood, and on that bloody field at the edge of their protectorate, the realm of Basilea was born, Bolisean becoming the first Hegemon of this new empire of men.

Since that day, Basilea has been the last shining bastion of humanity, the centre of man's power and learning, and the upholder of the traditions of Primovantor, in whose shadow it persists.

The Basileans

Being a people watched over by literal gods, the Basileans are both pious and conceited. It is difficult not to feel arrogant when one has beings of such power at one's back, and it is equally difficult not to have faith when your gods manifest physically before you. The Golden Horn is full of churches, and the faith holds great temporal power. It is through the Shining Ones power and guardianship that the Hegemony has persisted these last nine hundred years, and none of its people are soon likely to forget this.

Its position as a trade route and its importance as a central hub in human civilisation, combined with the reliance of smaller, satellite states on its protection, have seen Basilea grow rich and powerful. Though it may never truly rival the scale and sheer majesty of the old Primovantor, Basilea is undoubtedly one of the wealthiest nation states in all of Mantica.

Basilea's wealth means that its footsoldiers march to war clad in the finest plate and bearing the very best weapons that money can buy. Vast armies of them march to protect its borders, bolstered by the elite religious warriors of the Paladins on foot and atop mighty warhorses, and the fanatical Sisterhood, fighting on foot or riding to battle mounted on Gur Panthers or chariots pulled by these magnificent, if terrifying apex predators. Their warmachines are intricate and well built, and their magical support is second to none, Basilea having the highest concentration of magical colleges anywhere in the world.

With these forces alone, Basilea could endure for centuries as one of the great powers of Mantica. When the forces of the Shining Ones are added, the eternal supremacy of the Golden Horn is assured. Elohi march alongside the troops of Basilea, living manifestations of divine fury, each the equal of many dozens of men. It is no surprise that Basilea has become as arrogant as it is fervent. There are simply no powers in the world who can match it. For now.

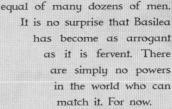

Men-at-Arms (sword & shield) Infantry

Unit Size	Sp	Me	Ra	De	Att	Ne	Pts
Troop (10)	5	4+	–	4+	10	10/12	80
Regiment (20)	5	4+	–	4+	12	14/16	115
Horde (40)	5	4+	–	4+	25	21/23	190

The backbone of the Basilean forces, the Men-at-Arms are the largest, and most highly trained standing army in Mantica. None can match their ranks for discipline of formation, nor tenacity in battle. Though the lowliest of the troops fielded by this great nation, they are its bedrock.

Men-at-Arms (spear & shield) Infantry

Unit Size	Sp	Me	Ra	De	Att	Ne	Pts
Troop (10)	5	4+	–	4+	10	10/12	95
Regiment (20)	5	4+	–	4+	15	14/16	135
Horde (40)	5	4+	–	4+	30	21/23	225

Special
Phalanx

Most common are units armed with the 'koliskos', a broad-bladed spear in use since before the age of the Republic, and with the simple but effective 'daga' sword. The soldiers are heavily armoured, clad in chain or scale mail depending on where they were raised and additionally protected by large winged shields often embossed with the sun emblem of Basilea.

Crossbowmen Infantry

Unit Size	Sp	Me	Ra	De	Att	Ne	Pts
Troop (10)	5	5+	5+	4+	8	10/12	100
Regiment (20)	5	5+	5+	4+	10	14/16	130
Horde (40)	5	5+	5+	4+	20	21/23	215

Special
Crossbows, Piercing (1), Reload!

The ever present threat of the Abyss and their swift-footed creatures means skill at arms is more prized than missile weaponry. But all that means is each shot must count, and the Basilean soldiers chosen to carry crossbows into battle are the best shots Basilea has to offer.

Penitents Mob Infantry

Unit Size	Sp	Me	Ra	De	Att	Ne	Pts
Troop (10)	5	5+	–	3+	10	8/10	70
Regiment (20)	5	5+	–	3+	15	12/14	100
Horde (40)	5	5+	–	3+	30	19/21	165

Special
Crushing Strength (1), Headstrong

Roving bands of lunatics, from deranged doom-sayers to zealots on absurd crusades.

Paladin Foot Guard Infantry

Unit Size	Sp	Me	Ra	De	Att	Ne	Pts
Troop (10)	5	3+	–	5+	10	11/13	105
Regiment (20)	5	3+	–	5+	12	15/17	150

Special
Headstrong

Options
• Exchange shields for two-handed weapons for free (lower Defence to 4+, gain Crushing Strength (1))

Armoured in heavy, ornate plate mail, the Paladins are also shielded by their faith. They exult in combat, nothing is more sacred to them than the blood of Basilea's enemies in the dust. They fight either on foot in the Paladin Guard or as Knight Paladins mounted on fiery barded warhorses. The Basilean Guard is the foremost elite infantry of the Basilean legions and the dismounted paladins use hefty two-handed swords to terrifying effect. But it is when mounted and using their famous long lances that the Paladins achieve their truly awesome battlefield potential – the Knight Paladins are amongst the most feared cavalry units in all of Mantica.

Paladin Knights Cavalry

Unit Size	Sp	Me	Ra	De	Att	Ne	Pts
Troop (5)	8	3+	–	5+	8	12/14	135
Regiment (10)	8	3+	–	5+	16	15/17	210
Horde (20)	8	3+	–	5+	32	22/24	350

Special
Headstrong, Thunderous Charge (2)

The mounted arm of the Basilean legions, Knight-Paladins thunder across battlefields astride huge, barded warhorses. There are few foes who can withstand their crushing charge, and any that do will have little time to regroup before they are set upon by the most well trained swordsmen in western Mantica.

Sisterhood Infantry Infantry

Unit Size	Sp	Me	Ra	De	Att	Ne	Pts
Troop (10)	5	4+	–	3+	10	10/12	90
Regiment (20)	5	4+	–	3+	15	14/16	130
Horde (40)	5	4+	–	3+	30	21/23	215

Special
Crushing Strength (1), Headstrong, Vicious

The convents of the Word are scattered across the countryside of Basilea, their nature obliging them to isolation. This remoteness means they must rely on themselves for their defence, and the Sisters spend as much time training their bodies as their soul. The Sisterhood will often lend their elite light infantry to nearby garrisons in times of need.

Sisterhood Panther Lancers — Cavalry

Unit Size	Sp	Me	Ra	De	Att	Ne	Pts
Troop (5)	10	4+	–	3+	8	11/13	115
Regiment (10)	10	4+	–	3+	16	14/16	175

Special

Nimble, Thunderous Charge (1), Vicious

The Gur Panthers of the Tarkis Mountains have long been used as mounts for the Sisterhood infantry of nearby convents. The semi-intelligent panthers are deadly hunters, and partial domestication has done nothing to dim their urge to chase down and devour prey.

Sisterhood Panther Chariot — Large Cavalry

Unit Size	Sp	Me	Ra	De	Att	Ne	Pts
Regiment (3)	9	4+	–	4+	15	12/14	180
Horde (6)	9	4+	–	4+	30	15/17	280

Special

Base Size: 50x100mm, Thunderous Charge (2), Vicious

Most of the orders eschew armour for speed and act as skirmishers, light cavalry, scouts and infiltrators. Their preferred weapons are heavy flails and the glaive, a curved variation on the koliskos, used whether on foot, mounted on Gur Panthers or even riding fast chariots pulled by these ferocious battlecats.

Heavy Arbalest — War Engine

Unit Size	Sp	Me	Ra	De	Att	Ne	Pts
1	5	–	5+	4+	1	10/12	65

Special

Blast (D3+2), *Reload!,* Piercing (3)

The one missile weapon seen more often in the ranks of the Hegemon's armies is the arbalest, a heavy crossbow. Of little use in fighting the fell creatures of the Abyss, detachments of arbalesteers are common in garrisons, as their armour-piercing bolts have proved invaluable in battling King Golloch's heavily protected dwarf warriors.

Elohi — Large Infantry

Unit Size	Sp	Me	Ra	De	Att	Ne	Pts
Regiment (3)	10	3+	–	5+	9	-/14	195
Horde (6)	10	3+	–	5+	18	-/17	300

Special

Crushing Strength (1), Fly, Inspiring, Thunderous Charge (1)

The Elohi are the angels of the gods, the mightiest of all Basilea's warriors, sent from the top of mount Kolosu to protect the land the Shining Ones have chosen as their own. The Elohi are beautiful beyond mortal understanding, tall and free of blemish. Wings sprout from their shoulders, gleaming armour of unknown metals clads their limbs. They wield swords and spears the like of which are reminiscent of the terrible weapons of the Wars with Gods.

Phoenix · Monster

Unit Size	Sp	Me	Ra	De	Att	Ne	Pts
1	10	3+	–	3+	3	14/16	165

Special

Breath Attack (10), Crushing Strength (1), Fly, Heal (6), Inspiring, Regeneration (4+)

The Phoenix is the symbol of Basilea; an emblem of rebirth, of holy fire and of blazing fury. These semi-magical birds are summoned by the mages of Basilea to fight with the armies of the Hegemon. There are a brave few heroes who utilise them as mounts, although elaborate spells of protection from fire must be performed before the Phoenix can be mounted.

Dictator · Hero (Inf)

Unit Size	Sp	Me	Ra	De	Att	Ne	Pts
1	5	3+	–	5+	3	13/15	90

Special

Crushing Strength (1), Individual, Inspiring

Options

• Mount on a Basilean warhorse, increasing Speed to 8 and acquiring Thunderous Charge (1) (+30 pts), and changing to Hero (Cav)

Wise and charismatic Dictators – generals drawn from the ranks of the priesthood, paladins, sisterhood, and even from lowly men-at-arms – draw up grand strategies to protect the lands of the Hegemon from harm. As they tend to be older men, they might not be the most powerful of warriors, but their presence on the field is nevertheless vital to guide the Basilean legions to victory.

Bearer of the Holy Icon · Hero (Inf)

Unit Size	Sp	Me	Ra	De	Att	Ne	Pts
1	5	5+	–	4+	1	10/12	55

Special

Individual, Inspiring

Options

• Mount on a barded horse, increasing Speed to 8 and Defense to 5+ (+20 pts), and changing to Hero (Cav)

Only the bravest and most virtuous amongst the young acolytes are given the honour of carrying into battle one of the Holy Icons of Basilea. These take many forms, from golden statues of a saintly hero or heroine of Basilean history, to battle-flags of renowned regiments.

Priest · Hero (Inf)

Unit Size	Sp	Me	Ra	De	Att	Ne	Pts
1	5	4+	–	4+	1	11/13	75

Special

Crushing Strength (1), Headstrong, Heal (3), Individual, Very Inspiring (Penitents only)

Options

• Bane-chant (2) for +15pts
• Mount on a horse, increasing Speed to 9 (+15 pts) and changing to Hero (Cav)

The clerics that follow the troops on the battlefield are fully able to defend themselves.

High Paladin
Hero (Inf)

Unit Size	Sp	Me	Ra	De	Att	Ne	Pts
1	5	3+	–	5+	5	13/15	130

Special
Crushing Strength (1), Headstrong, Heal (2),
Individual, Inspiring

Options
• Mount on a Basilean warhorse, increasing Speed
  to 8 and acquiring *Thunderous Charge (1)* (+30pts),
  and changing to Hero (Cav)

The High Paladins, supreme warrior-priests
of Basilea, armour themselves and take to
the field alongside their Paladin brothers.
They are powerful fighters, sustained by the
unquenchable fire of faith and filled with
burning desire to smite all evil from the face
of the world.

High Paladin on Griffin
Hero (Mon)

Unit Size	Sp	Me	Ra	De	Att	Ne	Pts
1	10	3+	–	5+	7	15/17	210

Special
Crushing Strength (2), Fly, Headstrong, Heal (2),
Inspiring

Griffons are magic-born creatures, roosting in
inaccessible mountain peaks. Only the iron will
of Paladins of the Word have ever managed to
tame these ferocious beasts.

High Paladin on Dragon
Hero (Mon)

Unit Size	Sp	Me	Ra	De	Att	Ne	Pts
1	10	3+	–	5+	9	17/19	310

Special
Base Size: 75x75mm, Breath Attack (10), Crushing
Strength (3), Fly, Headstrong, Heal (2), Inspiring

The High Paladins, supreme warrior-priest of
Basilea, armour themselves and take to the
field alongside their Paladin brothers, calling
upon the gods for their favour and might. They
are powerful fighters, sustained by the holy,
unquenchable fire of their faith and filled with
burning desire to smite evil with all of their
strength. Normally they ride into battle on
strongly-built chargers, but at times they can
mount upon large Dragons – ferocious flying
monsters that can only be tamed by the iron
will of a High Paladin.

Abbess
Hero (Inf)

Unit Size	Sp	Me	Ra	De	Att	Ne	Pts
1	5	3+	–	4+	4	12/14	90

Special
Crushing Strength (1), Headstrong, Individual,
Very Inspiring (Sisterhood only), Vicious

Options
• Mount on a panther, increasing Speed to 10 and
  acquiring Thunderous Charge (1) (+20pts), and
  changing to Hero (Cav)

The spiritual leaders of the Sistehood lead their
sisters from the front.

Abbess on Panther Chariot
Hero (Lrg Cav)

Unit Size	Sp	Me	Ra	De	Att	Ne	Pts
1	9	3+	–	5+	8	14/16	170

Special

Base Size: 50x100mm, Crushing Strength (1), Headstrong, Thunderous Charge (1), Very Inspiring (Sisterhood only), Vicious

A chariotful of sharp (or blunt) unpleasantness.

Ur-Elohi
Hero (Lrg Inf)

Unit Size	Sp	Me	Ra	De	Att	Ne	Pts
1	10	3+	–	5+	6	-/15	180

Special

Crushing Strength (2), Fly, Heal (3), Inspiring, Thunderous Charge (1)

The Ur-Elohi are the most powerful of these creatures, shining beacons of light and Good, flying high in the sky to guide the armies of Basilea and its allies against all Evil. These mighty arch-angels are occasionally tasked by a Shining One to lead a crusade in their name: then an Ur-Elohi would descend from the heavens to confer with the leaders of the mortals, offering his nigh-infinite knowledge and wise guidance, as well as taking active part in the battle, destroying the most dangerous enemy entities with his lethal flaming sword!

War-Wizard
Hero (Inf)

Unit Size	Sp	Me	Ra	De	Att	Ne	Pts
1	5	4+	–	4+	1	11/13	60

Special

Fireball (8), Individual

Options

- Lightning Bolt (3) for +25 pts
- Wind Blast (5) for +30 pts
- Mount on a horse, increasing Speed to 9 (+15 pts) and changing to Hero (Cav)

Basilea's world-famous Schools of Magic provide mages of every kind. Magic is an integral part of all walks of life: including battle, where war-wizards, masters of fire and weather spells, wreak havoc upon the foes of Basilea with inferno and lightning. In particular, through centuries of incessant warfare, magic has been found to be a potent weapon to counter the denizens of the Abyss, against which it seems to have a greater effect.

Gnaeus Sallustis [1] Hero (Lrg Cav)

Unit Size	Sp	Me	Ra	De	Att	Ne	Pts
1	9	3+	–	5+	7	15/17	190

Special

Crushing Strength (2), Headstrong, Heal (3), Inspiring, Nimble

Gnaeus Sallustis is the Grand Master of the order of Basilean Paladins. His appearance on the battlefield is bad omen for the enemies of Basilea, as no army he has lead has ever lost a battle. He rides into battle atop his gigantic Basilean lion, Nakir, cutting swathes through the enemy ranks to reach his ultimate objective, a final confrontation with the enemy general.

Jullius, Dragon of Heaven [1] Hero (Lrg inf)

Unit Size	Sp	Me	Ra	De	Att	Ne	Pts
1	10	3+	–	6+	8	-/16	275

Special

Crushing Strength (2), Fly, Heal (3), Thunderous Charge (1), Twin Souls, Very Inspiring

Samacris, Mother of Phoenixes [1] Hero (Lrg Inf)

Unit Size	Sp	Me	Ra	De	Att	Ne	Pts
1	10	3+	–	5+	3	-/15	230

Special

Fireball (10), Crushing Strength (1), Fly, Heal (7), Inspiring, Lightning Bolt (5), Regeneration (5+), Twin Souls

Twin Souls

As long as Samacris and Jullius are both present and in play on the table, they both have the Elite special rule.

Irdima was left alone on the battlefield, cradling the two parts of Fotia's corpse and weeping. Suddenly, by the great power of her words of love and her frantic prayers, a miracle manifested and the two halves did not die. Instead, one half; representing the cauterising, vengeful and warlike nature of fire, became the Ur-Elohi Jullius, the Dragon of Heaven, whilst the other half; the nurturing, renewing and cleansing nature of fire, returned as the Ur-Elohi Samacris, the Mother of Phoenixes. And so, the Shining One who was Fotia, was reborn as the Phoenix and the Dragon. Weaker now individually, they are more powerful united, and their story is told as a parable of the passion and indestructibility of love; their strength in unity, giving rise to sayings such as "You can't cut fire with a sword", meaning that two lovers are inseparable.

DWARF ARMIES

The ancient race of Dwarfs has long dwelled in subterranean holds, and trace their history back farther than any race but the Elves. In the oldest tomes in darkened halls, the Dwarfs record the legends of the first of their race, born of stone and tears. They believe the goddess of the underworld wept for her lack of children in a darkened cave, and over long ages those tears formed a stalactite in the semblance of what we now know as a Dwarf. The character of Dwarf-kind reflects this poetic myth – they are a race as strong and enduring as the rock they mine, and as passionate as the goddess who made them.

Dwarfs are tenacious, hardy and determined, possessed of physical strength and mental fortitude that makes them ideally suited for warfare and backbreaking work – both of which they not only excel at, but enjoy. For a Dwarf, the greatest rewards are those that can be earned through physical toil and martial prowess, and they go about these pursuits with grim seriousness. Though the average Dwarf stands less than shoulder-high to a man, they are immensely broad of back, barrel-chested and thick-skulled. A Dwarf's hands are large, with thick, strong fingers that belie their remarkable dexterity. Their heads are set forward from their shoulders, giving them a downwards countenance that contributes to their dour reputation, though other races comment unkindly that Dwarfs must always look down so as not to trip over their trailing beards and massive feet. Long hair trails from their heads, varying in shade from russet red to flaming orange, while their flinty eyes and hawkish noses speak volumes about their suspicious and insular character. For the Dwarfs, above all races, keep themselves to themselves. Before the time of King Golloch, the conqueror,

Dwarf Army Special Rules

Alignment: Good

Grizzled Veterans
All units in this list have the *Headstrong* special rule, unless specified otherwise.

Dwarven Throwing Mastiffs
The Dwarfs train a breed of war-dog that is infamous for being even more vicious and hard-headed than its creators.

Mark a unit that has been equipped with throwing mastiffs with one or more such model. The unit has a ranged attack with a range of 12" that can be used only once per game (remove the mastiff markers once the weapon is used up).

When you release the hounds, roll 5 dice to hit, regardless of the firer's Attacks. Dogs always hit on 4+ regardless of modifiers. Then, for each point of damage caused,

roll to hit and to damage again, as the surviving dogs savage the unfortunate opponents. Repeat this process again and again until you fail to score any damage, at which point even the toughest of the dogs have been put down or have run off to bury some of the enemies' limbs.

Against units with the *Shambling* special rule, you can re-roll any dice that fail to damage... the mastiffs are that keen.

it was rare for the Dwarfs to leave their strongholds. They mistrust other races, particularly Elves, with whom they have long shared the world, and instead look to gold and gems dug from their cyclopean mines for companionship and succour.

As can be expected of a race so obsessed with stone and wealth, Dwarfs are stolid and unyielding in almost all facets of their lives. Treaties signed with Dwarf kings have oft been invoked centuries later, when all the original signatories have long passed; wars have been fought over the refusal to uphold such pacts, even though none but the Dwarfs even remember the cause. Likewise, Dwarf merchants are infamous for their contracts, which will always be adhered to the letter, if not the spirit. It is no coincidence that Dwarfs often carve binding agreements into granite tablets, literally setting a bargain in stone so that none dare break it.

Dwarf craftsmen are renowned across Mantica for their great skill and ingenuity. The men of Basilea covet the services of Dwarf masons to bolster their fortresses and lay foundations for their expanding cities. In the mountain holds, Warsmiths experiment endlessly with new engines of war, their blackpowder weaponry and intricate clockwork devices prized by kings and petty warlords alike. Warsmiths live an almost monastic existence, their guilds more akin to temples, dedicated to the fire god who blesses their instruments of war and flows deep magic through their forges. In vast forges in deep volcanic chambers, Warsmiths create armour and weaponry that are the envy of the world. Every helmet and breastplate is perfectly tailored to its wearer, sturdier than any artefact forged by men or Orcs, and yet adorned with delicate gold icons and valuable jewels; every axe-head is etched with intricate runes and chased with precious metals. For a Dwarf, if something is worth making, it's worth making well. Every artisan, from the smiths to the masons, passes down his secrets and methods to his apprentices, ensuring that his unique creations will live on forever, embellished and improved upon in time-honoured tradition by those he trains.

Such commitment to craft developed in part because the Dwarfs lack a natural affinity to magic, which men and Elves have come to rely upon so much. However, there are a handful of Dwarfs born in every generation who stand apart from their kin, displaying an innate mastery over the element of earth. These Dwarfs are recognised by their tough skin and dark eyes, cutting solitary figures in the deepest halls, where they wander apart from their kin to converse with earth spirits. Their strange talents sometimes manifest themselves violently, causing them to become outcasts until others of their kind find them and induct them into the Order of Stone. Eventually becoming Stone Priests, these Dwarfs command the elements upon which Dwarf-kind has built its civilisation, summoning shambling Earth Elementals to fight alongside their hold's armies. They are a breed apart from their kin, rightly feared and respected in Dwarf society.

To outsiders, life in a Dwarf hold must seem grim, far away from the sun, and surrounded by dour miners and doughty soldiers. Yet this is far from the truth. The wealthiest holds are places of light and

warmth, with polished mirrors and gigantic lanterns illuminating vast underground cities of carven stone and glittering gold. Meat roasts on firepits in massive feasting halls; Dwarf ale – some of the strongest and finest beer to be found anywhere in the world – is consumed in huge quantities; songs of heroism and tragedy echo around the caverns, reminding the Dwarfs of glories past, and glories still to come. Though possessed of a serious disposition and prone to melancholy, Dwarfs are capable of great mirth and overwhelming passion. They are as wont to sing a saga or start a drunken brawl as they are to weep sincerely over the loss of an ancestor, for their long lives are cursed with long memories, and they feel pain and love and anger perhaps more keenly than a man. For some Dwarfs, such intense emotion is a way of life – the Berserkers of Cwl Gen struggle daily to overcome the 'red curse', the rage that they harness in battle.

To insult a drunken Dwarf is to take one's life into one's own hands, and yet to secure a friendship with a Dwarf – a thing most rare for a race so mistrusting of others –

is to secure a lifelong companion, and a defender to the death. A Dwarf's sense of loyalty to hearth and home, to kin and clan, knows no bounds, and for this he will fight and die without question or pause. It is this quality that makes the Dwarfs so feared in battle – they enter into no act of war lightly, but when they do they will never back down, never surrender, and never, ever forget.

Ironclad
Infantry

Unit Size	Sp	Me	Ra	De	Att	Ne	Pts
Troop (10)	4	4+	–	5+	10	10/12	75
Regiment (20)	4	4+	–	5+	12	14/16	110
Horde (40)	4	4+	–	5+	25	21/23	180

Options
• Dwarven Throwing Mastiff (+10 pts)

Solid and uncompromising as rock, units of Ironclads form the backbone of most Dwarf armies. Armed with axes or hammers and clad in heavy armour, these Dwarf warriors are tough, stubborn fighters, who form a nigh-unbreakable line of steel on the battlefield.

Ironguard
Infantry

Unit Size	Sp	Me	Ra	De	Att	Ne	Pts
Troop (10)	4	3+	–	6+	10	11/13	110
Regiment (20)	4	3+	–	6+	12	15/17	160

Options
• Exchange shields for two-handed weapons for free (lower Defence to 5+, gain Crushing Strength (1))
• Dwarven Throwing Mastiff (+10 pts)

The Ironguard comprises handpicked veterans and sworn protectors of the Dwarf lords. Chosen from the toughest and most experienced fighters, they form defensive shieldwalls upon which even the strongest enemies expend their strength harmlessly.

Shieldbreakers
Infantry

Unit Size	Sp	Me	Ra	De	Att	Ne	Pts
Troop (10)	4	4+	–	4+	10	10/12	90
Regiment (20)	4	4+	–	4+	12	14/16	130
Horde (40)	4	4+	–	4+	25	21/23	215

Special
Crushing Strength (2)

Options
• Dwarven Throwing Mastiff (+10 pts)

The strongest Ironclads go to war equipped with heavy, two-handed hammers, whose weight alone is enough to break bones and splinter shields with equal ease, earning the Shieldbreakers their name.

Bulwarkers
Infantry

Unit Size	Sp	Me	Ra	De	Att	Ne	Pts
Troop (10)	4	4+	–	5+	10	10/12	105
Regiment (20)	4	4+	–	5+	15	14/16	150
Horde (40)	4	4+	–	5+	30	21/23	250

Special
Phalanx

Options
• Dwarven Throwing Mastiff (+10 pts)

Trained to withstand enemy cavalry charges, and armed with long spears and thick armour, Bulwarkers are masters of close formation fighting, even when on the move.

Ironwatch Crossbows Infantry

Unit Size	Sp	Me	Ra	De	Att	Ne	Pts
Troop (10)	4	5+	5+	4+	8	10/12	100
Regiment (20)	4	5+	5+	4+	10	14/16	135
Horde (40)	4	5+	5+	4+	20	21/23	225

Special
Crossbows, Piercing (1), Reload!

The oldest (and, perhaps, fattest) Dwarf warriors are often assembled into the ranks of the Ironwatch. Most Dwarfs lose none of their wits or keenness of sight with venerable age, and thus take to battle armed with crossbow or blackpowder rifle, so they may fight from a more sedentary position.

Ironwatch Rifles Infantry

Unit Size	Sp	Me	Ra	De	Att	Ne	Pts
Troop (10)	4	5+	5+	4+	8	10/12	115
Regiment (20)	4	5+	5+	4+	10	14/16	155
Horde (40)	4	5+	5+	4+	20	21/23	255

Special
Rifles, Piercing (2), Reload!

Rangers Infantry

Unit Size	Sp	Me	Ra	De	Att	Ne	Pts
Troop (10)	5	4+	4+	4+	10	10/12	135
Regiment (20)	5	4+	4+	4+	12	14/16	180

Special
Light crossbows (treat as bows), Crushing Strength (1), Pathfinder, Vanguard

Options
• Dwarven Throwing Mastiff (+10 pts)

Dwarf Rangers are often young, vigorous Dwarfs, curious about the world outside the holds. Though greeted with suspicion by older, more traditional Dwarfs, Rangers are expert scouts, explorers and pathfinders, specialising in ambush warfare and flank marches.

Sharpshooters · Infantry

Unit Size	Sp	Me	Ra	De	Att	Ne	Pts
Troop (5)	4	5+	4+	5+	5	9/11	100

Special

Base Size: 25x50mm, Long rifles, Piercing (2), Reload!

Unlike the Ironwatch, Dwarf Sharpshooters are recruited from among the hardiest apprentices in the Warsmiths' guild-temples. Bringing the latest long-ranged blackpowder weapons to war, their units are one part deadly sniper regiment and one part experimental field-testers!

Berserker Brock Riders · Cavalry

Unit Size	Sp	Me	Ra	De	Att	Ne	Pts
Troop (5)	8	4+	–	4+	13	-/16	135
Regiment (10)	8	4+	–	4+	26	-/22	210

Special

Thunderous Charge (1), Vicious

Only a Berserker would be mad enough to trap and tame the vicious Brocks that inhabit vast warrens within the Dwarfs' realm. Securing such a steed is deemed a sign of courage and honour within the Berserker clans, and the blood-crazed cavalry charge to battle roaring their infamous warcry: "Go for Brock!"

Berserkers · Infantry

Unit Size	Sp	Me	Ra	De	Att	Ne	Pts
Troop (10)	5	4+	–	3+	20	-/16	125
Regiment (20)	5	4+	–	3+	25	-/22	180

For some Dwarfs, the tragic history of their people overwhelms the senses, bringing on the red curse that, in battle, transforms them into frenzied lunatics! Fighting with wild abandon and seemingly feeling no pain, Berserkers do not stop fighting until they fall down dead.

Earth Elementals · Large Infantry

Unit Size	Sp	Me	Ra	De	Att	Ne	Pts
Regiment (3)	5	4+	–	6+	9	-/14	130
Horde (6)	5	4+	–	6+	18	-/17	200

Special

Crushing Strength (1), Pathfinder, Shambling

Summoned to war by the mysterious Stone Priests, these supernatural creatures are formed of the very earth and rock of the Dwarf holds – the living embodiment of the mountains come to protect their people!

Greater Earth Elemental Monster

Unit Size	Sp	Me	Ra	De	Att	Ne	Pts
1	5	4+	–	6+	8	–/18	160

Special

Crushing Strength (3), Pathfinder, Shambling

These black-stone giants are massive constructs of impenetrable rock. When the power of such creatures is harnessed by the Stone Priests, what foe would dare stand in the path of the Dwarfs?

Ironbelcher Cannon War Engine

Unit Size	Sp	Me	Ra	De	Att	Ne	Pts
1	4	–	5+	5+	1	10/12	110

Special

Blast (D6+2), Piercing (4), Reload!

While within 6" of a Friendly Warsmith, the unit has Blast (D6+3) instead.

The Ironbelcher has seen continuous service for many centuries. The simplicity, durability and destructive power of the Ironbelcher makes it an enduring weapon of war.

Ironbelcher Organ Gun War Engine

Unit Size	Sp	Me	Ra	De	Att	Ne	Pts
1	4	–	5+	5+	15	10/12	85

Special

Range 24", Piercing (2), Reload!

While within 6" of a Friendly Warsmith, the unit also has the Elite special rule.

This five-barrelled cannon discharges its deadly payload in a tight spread, chewing through closely packed enemy formations.

Flame Belcher War Engine

Unit Size	Sp	Me	Ra	De	Att	Ne	Pts
1	4	–	–	5+	18	10/12	85

Special

Breath Attack (Att).

While within 6" of a Friendly Warsmith, the unit also has the Elite special rule.

This weapon belches gouts of flammable liquid over the Dwarfs' foes, consigning them to a horrible death. Despite its short range, it is the ultimate area-denial weapon due to its fell reputation.

Jarrun Bombard War Engine

Unit Size	Sp	Me	Ra	De	Att	Ne	Pts
1	4	–	5+	5+	1	10/12	110

Special

Blast (D6+3), Lob it!, Piercing (2), Reload!

Lob It!

The Bombard can be fired directly, as normal. Alternatively, you can choose to fire it indirectly, following the Indirect Fire special rule. When firing indirectly, the Bombard has a range of 60", but cannot be fired against targets within 12".

Created by Jarrun Iremonger of Cwl Gen, this revolutionary weapon has become highly prized by Dwarf commanders. The Jarrun Bombard can be fired directly into enemy ranks like a heavy cannon, or indirectly like a mortar, bypassing fortifications to hit vulnerable troops beyond.

Battle Driller Monster

Unit Size	Sp	Me	Ra	De	Att	Ne	Pts
1	4	4+	–	5+	D6+6*	10/12	70

Special

Base Size: 25x50mm, Height 1, Brutal, Crushing Strength (1), Individual

* Roll for the number of Attacks every time you resolve a melee.

The Dwarf Miners Guild has long used technological innovations to aid in its excavations. Some members of the guild take their drilling devices to battle, charging them into the enemy ranks with spectacularly unpredictable results.

Steel Behemoth · Monster

Unit Size	Sp	Me	Ra	De	Att	Ne	Pts
1	4	5+	–	6+	D6+20*	18/20	250

Special

Base Size: 50x100mm, Breath Attack (10), Crushing Strength (3)

*Roll for the number of Attacks every time you resolve a melee

These innovative fighting vehicles are powered by ingenious internal combustion engines fuelled by the black blood of the earth. Protected by thick metal plates and equipped with flame-spitting weaponry, they are a nightmare made manifest for the Dwarfs' enemies.

King · Hero (Inf)

Unit Size	Sp	Me	Ra	De	Att	Ne	Pts
1	4	3+	–	6+	5	13/15	120

Special

Crushing Strength (1), Individual, Inspiring

The noble rulers of Dwarf-kind come from ancient lineages, and inspire utter devotion in their people. With a lifetime of warmongering behind them, and bearing magical rune-encrusted weapons and armour, they are mighty warriors in their own right.

King on Large Beast Hero (Lrg Cav)

Unit Size	Sp	Me	Ra	De	Att	Ne	Pts
1	7	3+	–	6+	7	13/15	170

Special

Crushing Strength (1), Thunderous Charge (2), Inspiring

Giant rodents and other unnaturally large burrowing creatures make excellent mounts for high-ranking Dwarves.

Warsmith Hero (Inf)

Unit Size	Sp	Me	Ra	De	Att	Ne	Pts
1	4	4+	4+	5+	2	11/13	85

Special

Pistol, Crushing Strength (1), Individual, Inspiring (War Engines only), Piercing (1)

Keepers of the ancient Secrets of Steel, Warsmiths are master craftsmen whose guild-temples furnish the Dwarf armies with destructive war engines, and the finest weapons and armour. Their knowledge of mechanical devices and blackpowder weapons is without peer.

Army Standard Bearer Hero (Inf)

Unit Size	Sp	Me	Ra	De	Att	Ne	Pts
1	4	5+	–	5+	1	10/12	50

Special

Individual, Inspiring

It is the greatest, most solemn honour to carry one of the Dwarfs' revered banners to battle, and only the most loyal retainers of the noble houses are entrusted with this duty. These ancient banners are older than any living dwarf, often inscribed with the feats of one of the noble houses.

Ranger Captain Hero (Inf)

Unit Size	Sp	Me	Ra	De	Att	Ne	Pts
1	5	3+	4+	5+	3	11/13	90

Special

Light crossbow (treat as bow), Crushing Strength (1), Individual, Inspiring (Rangers only), Pathfinder, Vanguard

Not all Dwarf Rangers are young striplings – some of their calling never outgrow the call of the wild, or the thirst for exploration. These seasoned adventurers take to the field in the prime of life, using all their experience as pathfinders and huntsmen to savage the enemy from the shadows.

Berserker Lord Hero (Inf)

Unit Size	Sp	Me	Ra	De	Att	Ne	Pts
1	5	3+	–	4+	8	-/17	120

Special

Crushing Strength (1), Individual,
Inspiring (Berserkers only)

Options

• Mount on a Brock (+30 pts), increasing Speed to 8,
  gaining Vicious and changing to Hero (Cav).

Few Berserkers live long enough to amass wealth
and status, or even a hold of their own, but
those who do master the red curse are mighty
warriors indeed. Usually carrying a pair of
magical axes as a symbol of their power, they
are nigh-unstoppable killing machines in battle.

Sveri Egilax [1] Hero (Lrg Cav)

Unit Size	Sp	Me	Ra	De	At	Ne	Pts
1	8	3+	-	4+	10	-/19	240

Special

Crushing Strength (1), Elite, Inspiring,
Thunderous Charge (1), Vicious

Renowned as the most dangerous Dwarf
alive, Sveri Egilax is the Berserker King of
Cwl Gen. Often mounted upon the fearsome
and bad-tempered Helbrokk, Sveri's rage is
boundless, such that he has been known
to cleave through entire enemy regiments
single-handed!

Stone Priest Hero (Inf)

Unit Size	Sp	Me	Ra	De	Att	Ne	Pts
1	4	4+	–	5+	2	11/13	105

Special

Individual, Inspiring (Earth Elementals only), Surge (8)

Options

• Bane Chant (2) for +15 pts

Within the Dwarf holds, Stone Priests are
outsiders, for their innate mastery of earth
magic is treated with suspicion by all right-
thinking Dwarfs. In battle however, they
are capable of summoning and controlling
powerful Earth Elementals to smash apart the
Dwarfs' foes.

Herneas the Hunter [1] Hero (Inf)

Unit Size	Sp	Me	Ra	De	At	Ne	Pts
1	5	3+	3+	5+	3	12/14	140

Special

Skewerer, Crushing Strength (2), Individual, Inspiring (Rangers only), Pathfinder, Stealthy, Vanguard

Skewerer

The Skewerer is a magic crossbow that in rules terms is treated as a bow with Piercing (3).

Leader of the Hunt

If your army includes Herneas, you may upgrade one unit of Rangers to represent his handpicked Ranger patrol (+20 pts). This unit has the Elite and Stealthy special rules.

Herneas is a living legend amongst the Dwarfs, a solitary hunter who embodies the tenets of the Rangers' way of war – a master of stealth and ambush, and an unmatched warrior.

Garrek Heavyhand [1] Hero (Inf)

Unit Size	Sp	Me	Ra	De	At	Ne	Pts
1	4	3+	-	6+	5	14/16	150

Special

Warp Hammer, Shield of Miph, Individual, Inspiring

Warp Hammer

The bearer has Crushing Strength (3).

Shield of Miph

The bearer has Regeneration (6+).

Garrek, mightiest scion of the Heavyhand clan, is a Dwarf cursed by the sins of his forebears. His deeds are celebrated across the length and breadth of Mantica. In battle, his legendary hammer earns him more renown with each kill, though he can never atone for the shame of his ancestors.

"I'll be glad when this is over," Njorri Forkbeard grumbled. "My back's killing me."

"Aye, mine too," agreed Jorin. "It's these firebelchers. Too heavy. Not a patch on the old design."

"Maybe you're just getting too old," Guttri Half-nose chimed in. Njorri sniggered. Guttri was the oldest Dwarf in the regiment, his white beard tied about the waist to stop it tripping him over.

"Too heavy!" Jorin snorted. "And the sights are off, too. Not like in my day."

"In your day it'd be as like to explode in your hands as hit anything," Guttri scolded. "And think of the range. Marvellous what they can do with rifling these days."

A distant cheer went up across the battlefield.

"What was that?" Njorri asked. "Can't see anything from up on this hill."

"I think it was the Brocks charging in," Jorin said, squinting against the sun. "Won't be long now. There won't be much left for us."

"Spoke too soon," Guttri said, his joints clicking as he raised his firebelcher. Sure enough a dark shadow swept over head; more followed. Eagles, four of them, circling above, their grotesque riders eyeing up the Dwarf Ironwatch for a diving charge.

"Right, looks like we're up," said Njorri. "Ironwatch! Give 'em what for!"

The venerable Dwarfs clambered to their feet, and forty guns aimed skywards. With a sound like

thunder, they fired. When the smoke had cleared, three massive eagles lay dead at the foot of the hill, and another was flapping away from danger as fast as it could go. The Ironwatch cheered.

"Well, that's us done for the day," Njorri said. "And I told you the sights were off on these belchers."

"Come off it!" Guttri chided.

"Well, one of 'em got away, didn't he? Wouldn't have happened in my day."

ELF ARMIES

Of the three Noble Peoples of ancient times, the Elves are said to be the oldest. Their kind has raised great cities and woven magical works since even before the Celestians came to Mantica. Indeed, the oldest of the Elves maintain that their ancestors treated with the gods themselves, and brought them to the world to usher in a long age of peace, knowledge and prosperity to the land.

Those times are ended. The Elves now are a people in decline. Many of their ancestral lands are gone, all of the Western Kindred's holdings, bar the city of Therennia Adar, are lost to the sea; most of those of the Southern Kindred and a good deal of the Eastern Kindred's realm is buried beneath desert sands. Still, the Elves are mighty, masters of magic beyond compare. Since the fall of the Celestians, their mages have become the greatest in the world. Whatever an Elf turns his keen mind to, he masters – whether this be art, poetry, magic, science or war. As such, their armies are disciplined, as effective individually as they are as in ranks. Bows and spears are their favoured weaponry, and regiments equipped with such are deadly indeed.

An Elf is much more slender than a man, and tall, but deceptively strong. Their muscles are hard and supple, and they can perform athletic feats that other races could not attempt. Next to an Elf, the most skilled human dancer appears graceless and ungainly. They are beings of poise, uniformly beautiful, quick to laugh and quick to anger. They are long-lived and wise, and yet impulsive and capricious. They love to create, and bend much of their long lives to artisanship. As a result their arts are beyond compare, their sagas beautiful in the telling, their swords fine as they are sharp. The passing of the Elves' golden age has given many cause for regret, and some have become wracked with bitterness. Others are consumed by a sorrow so deep they die of it, or gripped by lassitude that

Elf Army Special Rules

Alignment: Good

Battle Hardened

All units in this list have Elite, unless specified otherwise.

Elven Sabre-Toothed Pussycat
Meeoww!

Mark a Hero that is accompanied by a sabre-toothed pussycat with an Elven cat model. The Hero has a ranged attack with a range of 12" that can be used only once per game (remove the cat once it has been unleashed).

This weapon can only be used against Heroes or Monsters, War Engines and Troops. The cat, with typical feline obedience, refuses to attack any body of troops larger than that.

When you send the cat to seek its prey, roll 5 dice to hit, regardless of the firer's Attacks. The cat always hits on 4+, regardless of modifiers, and has the *Piercing (1)* rule. Then, for any point of damage caused, roll to hit and to damage again, as the cat has its way with the victims. Repeat this process again and again until you fail to score any damage, at which point the cat has been slain or has wandered off to lick the gore off its paws.

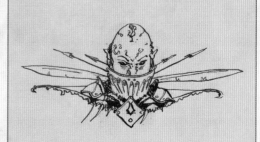

leaves them helpless for months. Many, particularly those of noble birth, have become adversarial to outsiders, aloof and proud. These flaws are understandable, for the Elves also bear terrible guilt, for they are responsible for much folly. It was the Elf Mage Calisor Fenulian who forged the mirror that caused the Sundering of the Celestials and destroyed the greatest civilisation in history. If that were not a heavy enough shame to bear, more recently their affection for a human youth, more skilled in the magical arts than any before him, blinded them to his propensity for evil, and so the necromancer Mhorgoth was unwittingly nurtured by their love, and instructed in arcane lore that even now he brings to bear upon the world.

Elves are born of the deep green places of the world, their primitive ancestors creeping out from under the boughs of the greenwood. Leaving the trees behind, they made the world their own, but always they have kept an affinity for nature wherever they dwell.

When the Celestians came to Mantica the Elves were readily adopted by the one known as the Green Lady, whom the Sylvan Kindred hold dear to this day.

The Kindreds

There are many Kindreds of Elves, ranging in size from small bands to entire nations consisting of varied clans and tribes. Many Kindreds have spent so long in isolation that they have adopted unique traits, both physical and cultural, making them virtual strangers even amongst other Elves. Listed here are the most renowned of the Kindreds of Mantica, though they are not the only ones.

The Northern Kindred

The most powerful of all the Kindreds, the Northern Elves count the Mage-Queen among their number. Ileuthar, the de facto capital of Elvenholme in these dark days, is their city, and the Twilight Glades grow upon their land.

The Sea Kindred

The lands of the Western Kindred in the far west are now sunk beneath the waters of the Great Ocean. Only the Brokenwall Islands and the City of Therennia Adar – known by Men as Walldeep – remains, saved by the sacrifice of Valandor the Great, although its Sacred Groves are drowned. The Western Kin are more commonly called the Sea Kindred or Sea Elves in this age, for those that remain have become masters of the oceans. Their thin-hulled ships skim like gulls over the waves. Their Sea Mages can sing up a storm, and command the mighty Kraken with but a word. These mariners furnish the Elven Kindreds with a powerful navy, and are known as the finest sailors in Mantica.

The Dragon Kindred

Only the Elves have ever truly mastered these ancient reptiles – the one legacy of Calisor to remain untarnished. The ties of respect and kinship that a dragon forms with an Elf are unsurpassed by other races. These bonds are so strong that should an Elven Dragon Lord die, his mount has

been known to pine such that it falls into an unnatural, grief-stricken slumber. Only an Elf truly worthy of replacing a dragon's rider can rouse the great beast from this sleep, and such Elves are rare. Once a tribe among the Northern Kindred, the Dragon Lords' power has grown out of all proportion to their Kindred's small size. Inhabiting the peaks of the Alandar Mountains, the Dragon Lords are an arrogant people, if noble to the core.

The Eastern Kindred

These Elves were once renowned as the most carefree of all. In their silk-covered wagons they roamed the savannahs of the east, making camp under the stars. The most talented musicians and poets were said to be of the Eastern Kindred, quick-witted and mirthful. Now they are a dour people, victims of the encroaching desert and the depredations of the Twilight Kindred, they are better known for bladecraft than poetry. The Drakon riders are their greatest warriors.

The Southern Kindred

Proud and haughty, the Southern Kindred defy the moving desert with magic and, when that fails, sheer stubbornness. Most of their cities are wind-blasted ruins, but the Elves remain in their tall towers, standing sentinel over the unending southern wastes. Much ancient lore is said to lie in the great libraries of the Southern Kindred, though their isolated realm has made the Elves there insular and unwilling to share their knowledge.

The Ice Kindred

Inhabitants of the Bitter Lands, masters of ice magic, the Ice Kindred are the most enigmatic of all Elves, even more reclusive and hostile to strangers than the Sylvan Kindred. Followers of the renegade King Tyris, they permit access to their lands infrequently, and travel rarely to the courts of the Twilight Glades and Walldeep. Of late, travellers north of the Mammoth Steppes have reported a court of Elves, believed by many to be a faction of the Ice Kindred. The Elves of Ileuthar know that this is not the case, however, and reports

of a fledgling Kindred gathering strength beyond the reach of Elevenholme has been met with much consternation.

The Sylvan Kindred

Living deep in the green places of the world, the Sylvan Kin are at one with nature. Long ago they rejected the ways of the other Kindreds, and fully embraced the arboreal origins of all Elves. They are antagonistic to any who would alter the natural order of the world, and have little contact with other races. Most dwell inside the bounds of the mystic forest of Galahir, but a large contingent live in Ileuthar, and several are the closest confidantes of Mage-Queen Laraentha.

The Twilight Kindred

Of these dark-hearted Elves, the other Kindreds will not speak to outsiders, but that they remain a part of wider Elven society is without doubt, for ambassadors of their kind are often found in Ileuthar. The Twilight Kindred are cruel and unforgiving, their hearts tainted by their proximity to the birth of the Wicked Ones during the Sundering. It is said that they believe themselves touched by the fallen gods, and thus fated to one day rule all of Elvenkind as masters.

Kindred Tallspears — Infantry

Unit Size	Sp	Me	Ra	De	Att	Ne	Pts
Troop (10)	6	4+	–	4+	10	10/12	100
Regiment (20)	6	4+	–	4+	15	14/16	140
Horde (40)	6	4+	–	4+	30	21/23	230

Special
Phalanx

Clad in fine Elven armour and carrying the long spears that are their namesake, Tallspears are trained in defensive warfare from an early age. Highly regimented, these Elven militia form a solid line at the heart of any Elf army.

Therennian Sea Guard — Infantry

Unit Size	Sp	Me	Ra	De	Att	Ne	Pts
Regiment (20)	6	4+	5+	4+	12	14/16	170
Horde (40)	6	4+	5+	4+	25	21/23	280

Special
Bows, Phalanx

Trained to fight on the upper decks of the Elven navy's sleek ships, the highly flexible Sea Guard are equipped to fulfil the roles of both tallspear and archer, an ability that makes them the most adaptable unit in the Elven army.

Palace Guard — Infantry

Unit Size	Sp	Me	Ra	De	Att	Ne	Pts
Troop (10)	6	3+	–	4+	10	11/13	105
Regiment (20)	6	3+	–	4+	12	15/17	150

Special
Crushing Strength (1)

The most experienced and skilled Elf warriors are drafted into the Palace Guard, where they swear their lives to the service of their lord. They wear the finest enchanted armour and fight with long glaives or two-handed blades, wielding them with impossible speed and elegance.

Kindred Archers — Infantry

Unit Size	Sp	Me	Ra	De	Att	Ne	Pts
Troop (10)	6	5+	4+	4+	8	10/12	115
Regiment (20)	6	5+	4+	4+	10	14/16	150
Horde (40)	6	5+	4+	4+	20	21/23	250

Special
Bows

Elven tactics rely heavily on shooting a deadly rain of arrows into the advancing enemies, to thin their numbers before the clash, or even to completely annihilate them before they can make contact.

Kindred Gladestalkers · Infantry

Unit Size	Sp	Me	Ra	De	Att	Ne	Pts
Troop (10)	6	4+	4+	3+	8	10/12	130
Regiment (20)	6	4+	4+	3+	10	14/16	175

Special

Bows, Pathfinder, Vanguard

Elves are renowned across Mantica as woodsmen and pathfinders without peer. The Gladestalkers are exemplars of these skills, living solitary lives guarding the great forest trails. In times of war they gather into regiments, scouting ahead of the Elf force and loosing hails of deadly arrows from the cover of the woods.

Forest Shamblers · Large Infantry

Unit Size	Sp	Me	Ra	De	Att	Ne	Pts
Regiment (3)	6	4+	–	5+	9	–/14	125
Horde (6)	6	4+	–	5+	18	–/17	190

Special

Crushing Strength (1), Pathfinder, Shambling, Vanguard. This unit is not Elite.

Unstoppable constructs of wood, foliage, mud and stone, these great trees march against the enemies of the Elven realms. Though slow to anger, when awoken they are mighty and determined defenders of their woodland homes.

Hunters of the Wild · Infantry

Unit Size	Sp	Me	Ra	De	Att	Ne	Pts
Troop (10)	6	4+	–	4+	20	10/12	135
Regiment (20)	6	4+	–	4+	25	14/16	190

Special

Vanguard, Pathfinder. This unit is not Elite.

Like a true force of nature, wild and untamed, the fey creatures of the forest gather in great hunting bands when the Elves march to war, honouring ancient pacts between the Sylvan Kindred and the Green Lady. Gnomes, fauns, will o' the wisp, dryads and sprites form packs of spiteful warriors, fighting with the full fury of the Great Wild.

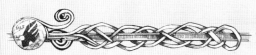

Stormwind Cavalry — Cavalry

Unit Size	Sp	Me	Ra	De	Att	Ne	Pts
Troop (5)	9	3+	–	5+	8	11/13	140
Regiment (10)	9	3+	–	5+	16	14/16	215

Special

Thunderous Charge (2)

The Elves breed horses that are noble of bearing and fast as quicksilver, elegant creatures that are deceptively strong and sturdy. In battle, units of Stormwind Cavalry speed across the battlefield on these magnificent beasts, clad in shining armour and striking at the enemy where they least expect.

Drakon Riders — Large Cavalry

Unit Size	Sp	Me	Ra	De	Att	Ne	Pts
Regiment (3)	10	3+	–	5+	9	12/14	175
Horde (6)	10	3+	–	5+	18	15/17	270

Special

Crushing Strength (1), Fly, Thunderous Charge (1)

Drakons, or Cold Drakes, are smaller cousins of the great Dragons, who dwell in the ancestral lands of the Eastern Kindred. Easier to tame than a Dragon, Drakons are no less ferocious, and form units of fearsome, winged shock cavalry.

Silverbreeze Cavalry — Cavalry

Unit Size	Sp	Me	Ra	De	Att	Ne	Pts
Troop (5)	10	5+	4+	4+	7	11/13	145

Special

Bows, Nimble

These mounted scouts range far ahead of the Elf army on the march. Peerless horse archers, the Silverbreeze Cavalry form a swift-moving vanguard to harry the enemy's flanks and pick off vulnerable foes with deadly accurate bowfire and lightning-fast strikes.

War Chariots — Large Cavalry

Unit Size	Sp	Me	Ra	De	Att	Ne	Pts
Regiment (3)	8	4+	4+	4+	8	12/14	140
Horde (6)	8	4+	4+	4+	16	15/17	215

Special

Bows, Base Size: 50x100mm, Thunderous Charge (2)

The Eastern and Southern Kindreds are famed for their chariot races, and often compete in this dangerous sport during the Elfmoots. In battle, chariots are pressed into service as devastating shock troops, pulled by swift Elven steeds.

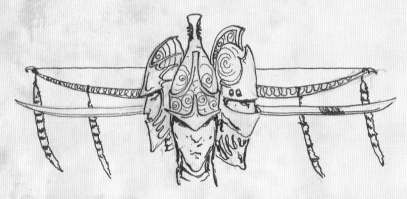

Bolt Thrower — War Engine

Unit Size	Sp	Me	Ra	De	Att	Ne	Pts
1	6	–	4+	4+	2	10/12	90

Special

Blast (D3), Piercing (2), Reload!

These powerful war machines hurl bolts as tall as a man with such force that they can level castle walls or skewer half a dozen knights with a single shot. They are quick to load and fire, and light enough that they can be swiftly moved around the battlefield, rapidly redeploying wherever their firepower is required.

Dragon Breath — War Engine

Unit Size	Sp	Me	Ra	De	Att	Ne	Pts
1	6	–	4+	4+	15	10/12	90

Special

Breath Attack (Att)

Such is the heat of the inferno unleashed by the Dragon's Breath that it is able to melt armour and flesh, making this ensorcelled war machine one of the most feared weapons on the field of battle.

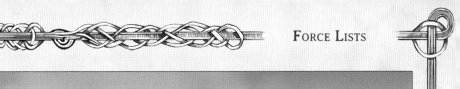

Elven King — Hero (Inf)

Unit Size	Sp	Me	Ra	De	Att	Ne	Pts
1	6	3+	–	5+	5	13/15	120

Special

Crushing Strength (1), Individual, Inspiring

Options

• Mount on a horse, increasing Speed to 9 (+20 pts) and changing to Hero (Cav)

• Sabre-Toothed Pussycat (+10 pts)

Amongst the ranks of Elven warhosts, there are those whose deeds have become as legend. These are the war-leaders of the Elven kings. Peerless warriors and masters of battlefield strategy, they have honed their killing arts over centuries of warfare.

Drakon Rider Lord — Hero (Lrg Cav)

Unit Size	Sp	Me	Ra	De	Att	Ne	Pts
1	10	3+	–	5+	5	13/15	160

Special

Crushing Strength (1), Fly, Inspiring, Thunderous Charge (1),

Lords of the Eastern Kindreds often ride to battle atop fierce Cold Drakes, striking where the enemy least expects. Often they circle the battlefield in ominous packs with their fellow Kindred, a portent of doom for the unwitting foe.

Dragon Kindred Lord — Hero (Mon)

Unit Size	Sp	Me	Ra	De	Att	Ne	Pts
1	10	3+	–	5+	10	17/19	310

Special

Breath Attack (15), Crushing Strength (3), Fly, Inspiring

The ancient pact between Elf and Dragon is a bond stronger than any treaty writ on paper or carved into stone. It is a symbiotic relationship, written in magic, fire and blood. Those Elven Lords who ride into battle atop one of these mighty beasts are powerful indeed, for when the will of an Elf and the strength of a Dragon unite, few can stand before them.

Elven Prince — Hero (Inf)

Unit Size	Sp	Me	Ra	De	Att	Ne	Pts
1	6	3+	–	5+	3	11/13	60

Special

Crushing Strength (1), Individual

Options

• Mount on a horse, increasing Speed to 9 (+15 pts) and changing to Hero (Cav)

• Sabre-Toothed Pussycat (+10 pts)

The nobles of the Elven courts often fill their youth with martial feats, practising swordplay and learning strategy for what would be a lifetime for a Man. These princes are great assets on the battlefield, though they can be headstrong, vying with each other for feats of heroism.

Noble War Chariot — Hero (Lrg Cav)

Unit Size	Sp	Me	Ra	De	Att	Ne	Pts
1	8	3+	4+	4+	4	11/13	90

Special

Bow, Base Size: 50x100mm, Thunderous Charge (2)

Champions of the arena and noble of birth, those princes and lordlings of the Elven court who ride to battle in a War Chariot are fortune-seekers and thrill-hunters, yet accomplished warriors all.

Army Standard Bearer — Hero (Inf)

Unit Size	Sp	Me	Ra	De	Att	Ne	Pts
1	6	5+	–	4+	1	10/12	50

Special

Individual, Inspiring

Options

• Mount on a horse, increasing Speed to 9 (+15 pts) and changing to Hero (Cav)

Usually drawn from long-serving champions of the Palace Guard, it is a singular honour to carry the army standard into battle. Bearing ancient enchantments of protection, the standards of the Elven Lords are an blessing to their warriors and an anathema to the forces of evil.

Elven Mage — Hero (Inf)

Unit Size	Sp	Me	Ra	De	Att	Ne	Pts
1	6	5+	–	4+	1	10/12	75

Special

Heal (3), Individual

Options

• Lightning Bolt (5) for +45 pts
• Wind Blast (5) for +30 pts
• Fireball (10) for +10 pts
• Bane Chant (2) for +15 pts
• Mount on a horse, increasing Speed to 9 (+15 pts) and changing to Hero (Cav)
• Sabre-Toothed Pussycat (+10 pts)

Among the most powerful wizards in Mantica, Elven Mages are inducted into the arcane mysteries at an early age. Able to harness the raw power of the elements, and protected by powerful wards, they are masters of battlefield spellcraft.

Master Hunter — Hero (Inf)

Unit Size	Sp	Me	Ra	De	Att	Ne	Pts
1	7	3+	3+	4+	3	11/13	90

Special

Bow, Individual, Pathfinder, Piercing (1), Stealthy, Vanguard

Options

• Sabre-Toothed Pussycat (+10 pts)

For some Elves, life at court is interminable, and they become filled with a wanderlust that takes them far from their kin. Alone in the trackless forests, many become Gladestalkers, while a few, often exile-princes of noble bearing, become masters of the beasts, often found upon the battlefield accompanied by massive sabre-toothed Lyrynx.

Forest Warden — Hero (Lrg Inf)

Unit Size	Sp	Me	Ra	De	Att	Ne	Pts
1	6	4+	–	5+	3	11/13	75

Special
Crushing Strength (2), Nimble, Pathfinder, Vanguard.
A Forest Warden is not Elite.

Though the Tree Herders are implacable and slow to anger, they are seen as headstrong and impatient by the ancient Forest Wardens. To provoke these massive woodland guardians to war is both an impressive feat and a dire mistake, for once angered they are nigh unstoppable foes.

Tree Herder — Hero (Mon)

Unit Size	Sp	Me	Ra	De	Att	Ne	Pts
1	6	3+	–	6+	7	18/20	260

Special
Crushing Strength (3), Inspiring, Pathfinder, Surge (8), Vanguard. A Tree Herder is not Elite.

The Tree Herders are mighty wooden giants that spend the long millennia of their lives protecting their forests from all threats.

Argus Rodinar [1] — Hero (Inf)

Unit Size	Sp	Me	Ra	De	At	Ne	Pts
1	0	-	–	5+	–	-/13	50

Special
Base Size: 50x50mm, Altar of the Elements, Individual

Altar of the Elements
Argus Rodinar treats all Wavering results as Steady and is never disordered by chargers – he is protected by powerful enchantments.

The Altar has a spell which automatically hits any one friendly non-allied unit on the battlefield, regardless of range or line of sight. Any nerve tests against this unit that result in a rout must be re-rolled, as if it were in range of an Inspiring unit. This spell lasts until the start of your next turn. Remember that dice cannot be re-rolled more than once.

As master of the Altar of the Elements, Argus Rodinar's duty is to balance the elements and forge victory from potential defeat, to manipulate the unseen forces of the world in an effort to ensure that victory lies with the servants of the Shining Ones.

The Green Lady [1] — Hero (Inf)

Unit Size	Sp	Me	Ra	De	At	Ne	Pts
1	10	–	–	6+	–	14/16	200

Special
Fly, Heal (8), Individual, Inspiring, Pathfinder, Regeneration (5+)

Options
• Up to 2 Sabre-Toothed Pussycats (+10 pts each)

The Wild Guard
If your army includes the Green Lady, for +20 points you may upgrade a single Regiment of Hunters of the Wild to represent the Green Lady's Wild Guard, her most devoted and sworn guardians. This unit has the Headstrong and Regeneration (5+) special rules.

A Celestian of ages past, given form as a being of the deep woods, the Green Lady has ever been revered by the Elves who inhabit the Galahir. Those who would defile the Elves' ancient forest realms must face the wrath of the Green Lady. She is at once the warm, summer sun and the howling winter gale; the giver of life and the reaper of souls.

KINGDOMS OF MEN

Of all the Noble Peoples, men are the most numerous. Men can be found everywhere, from the most verdant valley to the harshest environment, anywhere a living can be scratched from the land. In blazing deserts, the frozen north, jungle, plain and mountain, men dwell. They exhibit a bewildering array of outer forms and skin colour, and the palette of their emotions is equally as varied. Men can be black of heart or as pure as snow. Men have been known as great Elf Friends, men have been known to embrace and serve the Abyss willingly. Men are anything but predictable.

Kingdoms of Men Special Rules

Alignment: Neutral

Rallying Cry
All units in this list with the Inspiring rule have the Very Inspiring rule instead (already noted in their profile), including Inspiring granted by other means such as Magical Artefacts.

Men were once more inclined to good than they are now. The Republic of Primovantor was the apogee of human civilisation, a grand coalition of nations ruled by an elected senate and headed by the High Consul. The men of this time were long-lived and keen-minded. Nearly a thousand years after the republic collapsed, its feats of magic and art have yet to be matched. The Primovantians learned much from the Elves, and gave them much in return. From their mountain home of Primovantia, the early Primovantians brought as many lands into their Republic by diplomacy as by conquest. All citizens were treated equally under her laws, no matter whether they willingly joined or their country had been defeated in war, and it flourished because of it. Every man who fought for Primovantor did so willingly, to protect a land they were proud to call their own.

Winter's war finished the Republic, already severely weakened by the God War. The provinces north of the Dragon's Teeth mountains were ground to clay under the ice, its rich southlands drowned by the sea. Whereas once Primovantor was a mountain kingdom looking over fertile plains, it is now a peninsula.

The memory of this noble state lives on in Basilea, the largest and most powerful

of today's nations. The Basileans are adherents of the Shining Ones, and large numbers of paladins, warrior monks and battle nuns are found in their armies. The angelic Elohi fly above the hosts of Basilea, lending their pure voices to the battle hymns of holy warriors, and their strength to the army's assault.

The Successor Kingdoms are descended from Primovantor also, but the similarity to Basilea ends there, for they have been much influenced by admixtures of culture and thought from other lands and have followed their own path. There are as many as a hundred of these small statelets, ranging from independent cities to large dukedoms, and the genuine kingdom of Valentica. These small lands are in a constant state of rivalry. War between them is not uncommon. As a result of this the city-states are vital places, breeding brave men who range far in their ships.

In other places men live in conditions ranging from great culture to orcish barbarism, and everywhere in between. Dark Ophidia is the home of vile sorcery. To the far north, hordes of horsemen fight over the herds of mammoth and bison with Goblins. On the icy seashores beyond the Bitter Islands, reavers set sail

in longships, raiding and trading as far south as Elvenholme and Basilea. Upon the contested plain of Ardovikia, new lands reclaimed from the ice's retreat are founded. Caravans of camels criss-cross the deserts of the south between desert oases and dry cities, bringing exotic wares from cultures so far afield what is known of them by the nations around the Infant Sea is more legend than fact.

Naturally, man's method of war differs from place to place. The Successor Kingdoms are the homes of engineers and wizard-scholars, and their armies reflect this. Gunpowder weapons such as cannon and primitive handguns are common there. Basilea also possesses this technology, but relies more on divine magic and armoured horsemen to win its wars, backed up by Griffins and the Elohi. All the kingdoms born from Primovantor's ruins favour blocks of pikemen, a weapon used for millennia.

The Ophidians can draw upon a wide range of troops from across their empire; including desert-horsemen, fierce tribal warriors from the green south and all manner of light troops suited for their harsh land, supported by heavy infantry and horse drawn from the Ophidian cities. The Ophidians also enslave desert spirits to fight for them, and make use of legions of undead skeletons.

The northern tribes are less disciplined, but formidable nonetheless. Whether steppe rider or sea raider, all are raised as warriors from childhood, and they are consequently skilled individual fighters.

As a whole, men have a somewhat ambivalent relationship with the other speaking races of Mantica. Several states have very close ties with the Elves, the Valenticans in particular, with two great Elven cities actually being part of it, and Elven quarters in every other city besides. Dwarfs live throughout man's lands, descendants of refugees from the fall of the northern holds and, more recently, King Golloch's reign. The northern tribes sometimes make common cause with the Orcs or the Abyssal Dwarfs, or are else forced to fight for them as slaves.

The great alliances of the past may be fading memories, men are as likely to fight shoulder to shoulder with the Elves and Dwarfs as they are to oppose them, and on many occasions men have fought on both sides of the battle in these grand alliances.

Men however most often fight other men, whether through greed or hatred or honour or just through misunderstanding. Men are hot-blooded, and not always wise, their vivacity is a curse as much as it is a blessing.

Shield Wall
Infantry

Unit Size	Sp	Me	Ra	De	Att	Ne	Pts
Troop (10)	5	4+	–	4+	10	9/11	70
Regiment (20)	5	4+	–	4+	12	13/15	100
Horde (40)	5	4+	–	4+	25	20/22	165

These warriors are equipped with chain mail or leather armour and carry a sword or axe and a wide shield that they can lock together to adopt a defensive formation.

Foot Guard
Infantry

Unit Size	Sp	Me	Ra	De	Att	Ne	Pts
Troop (10)	5	3+	–	5+	10	10/12	95
Regiment (20)	5	3+	–	5+	12	14/16	135
Horde (40)	5	3+	–	5+	25	21/23	225

Options
• Exchange shields for two-handed weapons for free (lower Defence to 4+, gain Crushing Strength (1))

Human noblemen tend to equip the elite warriors making up their bodyguard with the best armour and weaponry that their wealth can afford.

Pike Block
Infantry

Unit Size	Sp	Me	Ra	De	Att	Ne	Pts
Regiment (20)	5	4+	–	3+	15	13/15	135
Horde (40)	5	4+	–	3+	30	20/22	225

Special
Ensnare, Phalanx

Some Human kingdoms train their spearmen to use very long pikes, losing the protection of their shields, but forming impenetrable hedgehogs.

Heavy Pike Block
Infantry

Unit Size	Sp	Me	Ra	De	Att	Ne	Pts
Regiment (20)	5	4+	–	4+	15	14/16	165
Horde (40)	5	4+	–	4+	30	21/23	270

Special
Elite, Ensnare, Phalanx

Guard infantry units equipped with very heavy plate mail and long spears.

Spear Phalanx
Infantry

Unit Size	Sp	Me	Ra	De	Att	Ne	Pts
Troop (10)	5	4+	–	4+	10	9/11	85
Regiment (20)	5	4+	–	4+	15	13/15	120
Horde (40)	5	4+	–	4+	30	20/22	200

Special
Phalanx

The most classic variant on the shield wall formation is a shield wall bristling with sharp metal-tipped spears.

Pole-Arms Block
Infantry

Unit Size	Sp	Me	Ra	De	Att	Ne	Pts
Troop (10)	5	4+	–	3+	10	9/11	70
Regiment (20)	5	4+	–	3+	12	13/15	100
Horde (40)	5	4+	–	3+	25	20/22	165

Special
Crushing Strength (1)

Strong Men armed with halberds, partisans, fauchards and other oddly-shaped poleaxes.

Militia Mob * Infantry

Unit Size	Sp	Me	Ra	De	Att	Ne	Pts
Troop (10)	5	5+	–	3+	10	8/10	50
Regiment (20)	5	5+	–	3+	12	12/14	70
Horde (40)	5	5+	–	3+	25	19/21	115
Legion (60)	5	5+	–	3+	30	25/27	170

Hurriedly conscripted in time of dire need, these rag-tag formations never last very long.

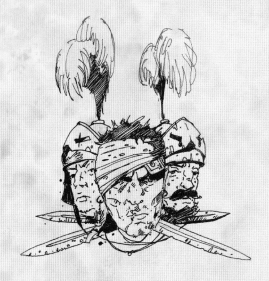

Bowmen Infantry

Unit Size	Sp	Me	Ra	De	Att	Ne	Pts
Troop (10)	5	5+	5+	3+	8	9/11	75
Regiment (20)	5	5+	5+	3+	10	13/15	100
Horde (40)	5	5+	5+	3+	20	20/22	165

Special

Bows

Bows are the most common ranged weapons in human kingdoms.

Crossbowmen Infantry

Unit Size	Sp	Me	Ra	De	Att	Ne	Pts
Troop (10)	5	5+	5+	3+	8	9/11	85
Regiment (20)	5	5+	5+	3+	10	13/15	115
Horde (40)	5	5+	5+	3+	20	20/22	190

Special

Crossbows, Piercing (1), Reload!

Some human rulers equip some of their troops with crossbows, trading tactical flexibility for hitting power.

Berserkers Infantry

Unit Size	Sp	Me	Ra	De	Att	Ne	Pts
Troop (10)	5	3+	–	3+	10	-/12	100
Regiment (20)	5	3+	–	3+	15	-/16	140
Horde (40)	5	3+	–	3+	30	-/23	230

Special

Crushing Strength (1)

Fur-clad norsemen with large axes and no fear of death.

Arquebusiers Infantry

Unit Size	Sp	Me	Ra	De	Att	Ne	Pts
Troop (10)	5	5+	5+	3+	8	9/11	100
Regiment (20)	5	5+	5+	3+	10	13/15	135
Horde (40)	5	5+	5+	3+	20	20/22	225

Special

Rifles, Piercing (2), Reload!

A relatively new weapon, hard-hitting arquebuses are an expensive replacement for crossbows.

Knights Cavalry

Unit Size	Sp	Me	Ra	De	Att	Ne	Pts
Troop (5)	8	3+	–	5+	8	11/13	125
Regiment (10)	8	3+	–	5+	16	14/16	195
Horde (20)	8	3+	–	5+	32	21/23	340

Special
Headstrong, Thunderous Charge (2)

Fanatical templars, brave knights on a chivalrous quests, or disinherited noblemen in search of redemption, these heavily armoured cavalrymen make fearsome shock troops.

Mounted Sergeants Cavalry

Unit Size	Sp	Me	Ra	De	Att	Ne	Pts
Troop (5)	9	4+	–	4+	7	10/12	105
Regiment (10)	9	4+	–	4+	14	13/15	160

Special
Nimble, Thunderous Charge (1)

Lightly armed compared with the knights, these swift cavalry units are used most often on the wings of a battle line, and to pursue and cut down enemies that are retreating from the battlefield.

Mounted Scouts Cavalry

Unit Size	Sp	Me	Ra	De	Att	Ne	Pts
Troop (5)	9	5+	5+	3+	7	10/12	100

Special
Bows, Nimble

Options
• Exchange bows with pistols for free (gain Piercing (1) but halve their range) or exchange bows with carbines for +15 pts (gain Piercing (1) and range 18").

These fast and flexible warriors form the eyes and ears of the army as it advances.

Charioteers Large Cavalry

Unit Size	Sp	Me	Ra	De	Att	Ne	Pts
Regiment (3)	8	4+	5+	4+	8	11/13	115
Horde (6)	8	4+	5+	4+	16	14/16	175

Special
Bows, Base Size: 50x100mm, Thunderous Charge (2)

Chariots are one of the most devastating weapons deployed by the Kingdoms of Men and only the finest warriors are permitted to use them. Training hard to acquire the expertise to handle the warhorses which draw them, as well as to gain the skill to make use of their weapons on the jolting shifting platform, charioteer units are the pride of any army, and the bane of any foe.

Cannon War Engine

Unit Size	Sp	Me	Ra	De	Att	Ne	Pts
1	5	–	5+	4+	1	9/11	85

Special

Blast (D6+1), Piercing (4), Reload!

The simplest and perhaps still the most cost-effective of war machines, the cannon is one Dwarf tradition that the Humans were very keen to make their own.

Siege Artillery War Engine

Unit Size	Sp	Me	Ra	De	Att	Ne	Pts
1	5	–	5+	4+	1	9/11	90

Special

Blast (D6+2), Indirect Fire, Piercing (3), Reload!

The most ancient of Human war engines, the Catapult is mostly used in sieges, but other more modern devices have appeared of lately, firing explosive shells or even rudimentary rockets in high arcs.

Ballista War Engine

Unit Size	Sp	Me	Ra	De	Att	Ne	Pts
1	5	–	5+	4+	1	9/11	60

Special

Blast (D3+2), Piercing (3), Reload!

A torsion-powered giant crossbow, whose bolts can easily skewer several enemy warriors.

Beast of War Monster

Unit Size	Sp	Me	Ra	De	Att	Ne	Pts
1	7	4+	–	5+	12	15/17	210

Special

Base Size: 50x100mm, Brutal, Crushing Strength (2), Thunderous Charge (2)

Options

• Mount a light ballista on it (+10 pts) – Range 36", Ra 5+, 2 attacks, Blast (D3), Piercing (2)

Large beasts of burden from the southern continents, armoured and sent into battle to smash and terrify the enemy.

General Hero (Inf)

Unit Size	Sp	Me	Ra	De	Att	Ne	Pts
1	5	3+	–	5+	4	12/14	100

Special

Crushing Strength (1), Individual, Very Inspiring

Options

- Mount on a horse, increasing Speed to 8 (+20 pts) and changing to Hero (Cav), or mount on a Pegasus, increasing Speed to 10 and gaining Fly, but losing the Individual special rule (+50 pts) and changing to Hero (Large Cav).

Human generals are not the most powerful warriors, but they are the best battle-leaders.

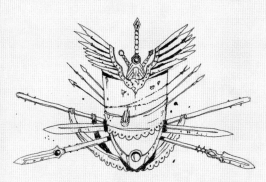

General on Winged Beast Hero (Mon)

Unit Size	Sp	Me	Ra	De	Att	Ne	Pts
1	10	3+	–	5+	6	14/16	190

Special

Crushing Strength (2), Fly, Very Inspiring

Only the richest noblemen can afford to ride a Hippogryph, Manticore or similar winged beast.

Hero Hero (Inf)

Unit Size	Sp	Me	Ra	De	Att	Ne	Pts
1	5	3+	–	5+	3	10/12	50

Special

Crushing Strength (1), Individual

Options

- Mount on a horse, increasing Speed to 8 (+15 pts) and changing to Hero (Cav), or mount on a Pegasus, increasing Speed to 10 and gaining Fly, but losing the Individual special rule (+40 pts) and changing to Hero (Large Cav).

These heroic knights are entirely absorbed with fulfilling a quest or other dangerous mission.

Army Standard Bearer Hero (Inf)

Unit Size	Sp	Me	Ra	De	Att	Ne	Pts
1	5	5+	–	4+	1	9/11	50

Special

Individual, Very Inspiring

Options

- Mount on a horse, increasing Speed to 9 (+15 pts) and changing to Hero (Cav)

Men are especially trained to follow the battle-signals issued by these large banners.

Wizard Hero (Inf)

Unit Size	Sp	Me	Ra	De	Att	Ne	Pts
1	5	4+	–	4+	1	10/12	50

Special

Fireball (6), Individual

Options

- Lightning Bolt (3) for +25 pts, or free if it replaces Fireball
- Wind Blast (5) for +30 pts
- Bane Chant (2) for +15 pts
- Heal (2) for +10 pts
- Mount on a horse, increasing Speed to 9 (+15 pts) and changing to Hero (Cav), or mount on a Pegasus, increasing Speed to 10 and gaining Fly, but losing the Individual special rule (+25 pts) and changing to Hero (Large Cav).

These lonesome, mysterious figures are a rare and powerful addition to any Human army.

The Captain [1] Hero (Inf)

Unit Size	Sp	Me	Ra	De	At	Ne	Pts
1	5	3+	–	5+	3	11/13	150

Special

Crushing Strength (1), Individual, Master Tactician, Very Inspiring

Options

- Mount on a horse, increasing Speed to 8 (+20 pts) and changing to Hero (Cav).

Master Tactician

You can redeploy D3 of your own units after deployment is finished, but before vanguard moves are made.

The Captain is the most seasoned of mercenary leaders. His services are expensive, but worth every copper coin.

FORCES OF NATURE

While the armies of Mantica wage constant war, vying for power in a tumultuous land, they are ever watched from the darkening forests and windswept tors. These secret watchers are the Druids, servants of the Green Lady, and they seek nothing more than true balance between the forces of light and darkness. When the scales tip too far in favour of good or evil, the Druids awaken their own armies – fey spirits, vengeful elementals and ferocious beasts – and march to restore order to the land. No leafy grove or befrosted tundra can provide sanctuary from the Forces of Nature; to battle them is to battle the world of Mantica itself.

It is said the Green Lady, the capricious being worshipped as a goddess by the Druids, is a Celestian, unique in her nature. She is a being composed of good and evil facets, and yet is neither one nor the other. She is in fact a tri-form entity, born of a fusion between a Celestian, a Wicked One and a Shining One, conflicting aspects that can be at peace, or at war, seemingly upon a whim, changeable as the weather.

When her Shining Aspect surfaces, the Green Lady is a gentle being, an avatar of the soothing, healing aspects of nature. In this form, she is oft worshipped by the Elves, who see in her the divinity of the woodland realms. Yet as much as this aspect is benign, the Wicked One within her can surface unpredictably, and woe betide any who are near when it does.

With this sudden change comes the harsh, feral reality of nature, red in tooth and claw. The urge to hunt, and to kill, which lies within the heart of all living things, is embodied by the Green Lady's Wicked Aspect. At her command, thorned elementals, monstrous beasts and spiteful creatures lope and slither from every forest, mountain-pass and seabound cove, intent on destruction of the Lady's foes.

Forces of Nature Special Rules

Alignment: Neutral

Creatures of Nature
All units in this list have the *Pathfinder* special rule, unless specified otherwise.

Wild Companions
A Wild Companion is a feral animal that is bound by magical means to a Druid or other master of the natural lore, or simply allied or in thrall to a particular race or creature.

Mark units that are accompanied by a Wild Companion with a suitable model – a panther, bear, wolf, hawk, etc. The unit then can unleash the beast once per game. This is the same as using a Fireball (5) spell with Piercing (1) – remove the animal model once it has been unleashed.

Ruling over these conflicting aspects is the Green Lady's Celestian heart, which strives for balance and equilibrium in all things. This, her aspect of 'The Preserver', is worshipped across Mantica by simple folk and nature spirits of the deep woodland, impenetrable marshes, vast prairies, icy tundra and scorched deserts. In this form, the Green Lady brings harmony to – and draws strength from – the four essential elements: earth, air, fire and water. She strives to use these elements to balance the struggle between good and evil, for her greatest fear is that one or the other will one day rule supreme over the world, and part of her own soul will be vanquished forever. If good were to prevail, the world would risk eternal stagnation. If evil reigned eternal, violence and destruction would tear Mantica apart.

Thus, the Lady is torn between her own aspects, and constantly allies herself with the weakest side, in an attempt to bring balance to the course of the eternal war. In recent years, Mantica has seen the rise of evil, and as such the Lady's Shining Aspect has dominated her own persona as she seeks to restore neutrality, and this stance has led to her forming great bonds with the Elves, who offer fealty in exchange for her sacred blessings.

To aid in her goals, the Green Lady calls upon mortal followers – lowly worshippers elevated to positions of power within the natural realm. These followers – the Druids – take the form of wandering priests, travelling the byroads and forest trails, spying on the races of man, Elf and Dwarf, observing from afar their successes and failures. When a Druid senses that the balance of power might be tipped –that a conquering army has grown too powerful, or a last bastion of one alignment is about to be overrun – they send word to the Green Lady, their goddess. Birds, Sylphs, insects, Naiads and sprites carry the Druid's message across land, sea and air, until it reaches the sacred groves of Galahir, where

the Lady's power is strongest. Here, the Druid Elders assemble in the Greenmoot, and combine their power to awaken the Lady and send her forces into battle. Her reach is long indeed, and at her unspoken command an army of monstrous creatures, fiery elementals and sylvan kin can strike many hundreds of leagues away.

Though the Druids are a secretive cult, and possess great power, the honour of joining their order is usually reserved for men, rather than the elder races. Other races are often more strongly aligned to the Shining Ones or the Wicked Ones, while man has ever been dynamic in his motives, open-minded and, some might say, malleable and easily swayed. Neither inherently evil or good, the race of men makes the best recruits for the Druid order, training for many years within the sacred bowers of the Green Lady to harness the power of the elements, and summon powerful creatures to the battlefield. Just as they must be careful to bring balance between the forces of good and evil, the Druids must also be mindful not to rely too heavily on one of the four elements, lest discord be struck within the natural order. As such, the backbone of any army marching at the command of a Druid will comprise Centaurs, children of the earth; Sylphs, the spirits of air; Salamanders, born of fire; and Naiads, daughters of water. Around these hordes of inhuman warriors flock gigantic eagles, supernatural ethereals, walking trees, fairy folk, and horrifying constructs that embody the spirits of nature itself.

The rise of the Lady's forces in recent times has given pause to many a warlord, who know that to extend their reach is to anger the spirits of Mantica. Even the greatest warriors tremble when the forests around them start to shake with sentient malice, the ground beneath their feet cracks with grim purpose, unnatural stormclouds gather overhead, and creatures of fire burst to life in the midst of their army. When the sound of fey hunting horns hangs on the breeze, and chill winds blast the serried ranks of invading forces, all know that the spirits of the wild have come, and they will show no mercy.

Naiad Ensnarers — Infantry

Unit Size	Sp	Me	Ra	De	Att	Ne	Pts
Troop (10)	5	4+	–	3+	10	9/11	100
Regiment (20)	5	4+	–	3+	12	13/15	140
Horde (40)	5	4+	–	3+	25	20/22	230

Special
Ensnare, Regeneration (4+)

Flitting between alluringly beautiful and terrifyingly ferocious, Naiads draw power from the water. As long as they are near to the ocean, a river, or even an underground spring, they can regenerate the most grievous wounds.

Naiad Heartpiercers — Infantry

Unit Size	Sp	Me	Ra	De	Att	Ne	Pts
Troop (10)	5	5+	4+	3+	8	9/11	120
Regiment (20)	5	5+	4+	3+	10	13/15	160

Special
Harpoon-gun, Piercing (1), Regeneration (4+)

In cruel mockery of the seafarers who have long invaded their ocean realm, preying on sea creatures, Naiad Heartpiercers carry heavy harpoon-launchers. Blessed with incredible longevity, Naiads spend several lifetimes practising with these weapons, becoming preternaturally deadly shots.

Naiad Wyrmriders — Large Cavalry

Unit Size	Sp	Me	Ra	De	Att	Ne	Pts
Regiment (3)	8	3+	–	4+	9	12/14	155
Horde (6)	8	3+	–	4+	18	15/17	240

Special
Crushing Strength (1), Regeneration (4+),
Thunderous Charge (1)

Riding upon supernatural sea serpents, Naiads add their spite and fury to the charge of their ferocious mounts. Though their powers are limited out of water, these great sea-wyrms are carried into battle on currents of magic for a limited time – which is usually all they need to smash asunder the enemy ranks.

Hunters of the Wild — Infantry

Unit Size	Sp	Me	Ra	De	Att	Ne	Pts
Troop (10)	6	4+	–	4+	20	10/12	135
Regiment (20)	6	4+	–	4+	25	14/16	190

Special
Vanguard

Spirits and faery folk of the forest realms, these creatures can assume many guises – fauns, dryads, sprites and will-o'-the-wisp. Although shy and peaceful in nature, if their forest realm is threatened, or by the command of their sylvan lords, they can be summoned in great numbers, assuming a frightening war-like aspect and fighting with the unbridled fury of the Great Wild.

Centaur Bray-Striders   Cavalry

Unit Size	Sp	Me	Ra	De	Att	Ne	Pts
Troop (5)	8	3+	–	4+	6	11/13	100
Regiment (10)	8	3+	–	4+	12	14/16	155

Special
Crushing Strength (1), Thunderous Charge (1)

Simple creatures of the earth, centaurs have the hind quarters of a horse and the upper body of a man. They are strong and powerfully built, and form swift, savage warbands of hunters when provoked, taking to the field with heavy two-handed swords or clubs.

Centaur Bray-Hunters   Cavalry

Unit Size	Sp	Me	Ra	De	Att	Ne	Pts
Troop (5)	8	4+	5+	3+	6	11/13	105
Regiment (10)	8	4+	5+	3+	12	14/16	165

Special
Bows, Nimble, Thunderous Charge (1)

Though not especially bright, Centaurs are naturally adapted for hunting, with their keen eyesight and impressive speed and stamina allowing them to stalk prey over long distances and bring them down with powerful bows. In battle, these skills make Bray-Hunters as formidable as any horse-archer in all Mantica.

Salamanders   Infantry

Unit Size	Sp	Me	Ra	De	Att	Ne	Pts
Troop (10)	5	4+	–	5+	10	10/12	100
Regiment (20)	5	4+	–	5+	12	14/16	140
Horde (40)	5	4+	–	5+	25	21/23	230

Special
Base Size: 25x25mm, Crushing Strength (1)

Options
• Exchange shields for two-handed weapons for free (lower Defence to 4+, gain Crushing Strength (2))

The Salamanders are an ancient race of reptilian fire-people, whose scaly red hides protect them from enemy weaponry as well as grant them a fearsome appearance. Their blood burns with great heat, manifesting in billowing vapours that exude from their fanged mouths, and channelling through their crude weapons, which sear and burn as well as they cut and crush.

Sylph Talonriders *   Large Cavalry

Unit Size	Sp	Me	Ra	De	Att	Ne	Pts
Regiment (3)	10	4+	4+	3+	6	12/14	135
Horde (6)	10	4+	4+	3+	12	15/17	210

Special
Bows, Fly

Few would dare to ride the massive eagles of the high peaks to war, for they are proud and savage creatures, with a keen intellect and regal bearing. However, they hold a close kinship with the Sylphs of the air, with whom they fight as an almost symbiotic pairing of ripping talons and deadly archery.

Forest Shamblers — Large Infantry

Unit Size	Sp	Me	Ra	De	Att	Ne	Pts
Regiment (3)	6	4+	–	5+	9	-/14	125
Horde (6)	6	4+	–	5+	18	-/17	190

Special

Crushing Strength (1), Shambling, Vanguard.

Unstoppable constructs of wood, foliage, mud and stone, Forest Shamblers are ancient spirits, roused from long slumber by the incantations of the Druids. Though slow to anger, when awoken they are mighty and determined defenders of their woodland homes.

Hydra — Monster

Unit Size	Sp	Me	Ra	De	Att	Ne	Pts
1	6	4+	–	5+	5*	15/17	140

Special

Crushing Strength (2), Regeneration (5+)

*Multiple heads – in addition to the basic 5, the Hydra has a number of additional attacks equal to its current points of Damage.

Found deep in mist-wreathed swamps, Hydras are thought to be immortal, and are almost unbeatable in combat. Their massive, reptilian forms and great strength make them formidable enough, but when one of their many heads is severed, two more grow back at once to take its place!

Beast of Nature — Monster

Unit Size	Sp	Me	Ra	De	Att	Ne	Pts
1	7	3+	–	5+	5	15/17	130

Special

Crushing Strength (2)

Options

- Lightning Bolt (6) for +30pts
- Breath Attack (10) for +15pts
- Fly and Speed 10 for +50pts
- Vicious and increase Attacks to 7 for +30pts

The origins of these monstrosities is known only to the Druid Elders, though they are rumoured to have been created during a violent episode of the Lady's Wicked Aspect. Terrifying to behold, they combine the most formidable traits of Chimera, Sphinx, Manticore and other monsters besides, forming a patchwork avatar of nature's wrath.

Elementals Large Infantry

Unit Size	Sp	Me	Ra	De	Att	Ne	Pts
Regiment (3)	5	4+	–	5+	9	-/14	130
Horde (6)	5	4+	–	5+	18	-/17	200

Special

Crushing Strength (1), Shambling.

Options

MUST take one of the following options:

- Earth: become De 6+ for free
- Fire: become Sp 6 and Crushing Strength (2) for free
- Air: become Sp 10 and gain Fly, but lose Crushing Strength for +20pts
- Water: become Sp 7 and gain Regeneration (5+) for +20pts

Unbridled spirits, Elementals are entities of raw energy, bound together by the magic of the Druids and the will of the Green Lady. Taking the form of goliaths of rock and dirt, swirling tornados, warriors of fire and lava, and sentient tidal-waves, their fury is unmatched on the battlefield.

Greater Elemental Monster

Unit Size	Sp	Me	Ra	De	Att	Ne	Pts
1	5	4+	–	5+	8	-/18	160

Special

Crushing Strength (2), Shambling

Options

MUST take one of the following options:

- Earth: become De 6+ and Crushing Strength (3) for free
- Fire: become Sp 6 and Crushing Strength (4), and gain Breath Attack (6) for free
- Air: become Sp 10 and gain Fly and Wind Blast (3) but reduced to Crushing Strength (1) for +30pts
- Water: become Sp 7 and gain Regeneration (5+) for +30pts

When the need is very great, the Elder Druids may unite to summon a Greater Elemental to battle. These towering behemoths loom large over the battlefield, like walking mountains, living thunderstorms, monstrous sentinels of flames, or aqueous giants.

Druid
Hero (Inf)

Unit Size	Sp	Me	Ra	De	Att	Ne	Pts
1	5	5+	–	4+	1	10/12	65

Special

Heal (2), Individual, Inspiring

Options

- Lightning Bolt (3) for +20pts
- Wind Blast (5) for +30pts
- Surge (7) for +40pts
- Bane-chant (2) for +15pts
- Can ride a stag, horse, lesser unicorn or similar mount, increasing Speed to 9, for +15 pts and changing to Hero (Cav)
- Up to two Wild Companions (+10 pts each)

Wandering abroad as the mortal eyes and ears of the Green Lady, Druids are powerful and mysterious men with a deep affinity for nature. Their burden is great, for at their command the guardians of Mantica will rise up from the wild places, and march to war.

Forest Warden
Hero (Large Inf)

Unit Size	Sp	Me	Ra	De	Att	Ne	Pts
1	6	4+	–	5+	3	11/13	75

Special

Crushing Strength (2), Nimble, Vanguard

Though the Tree Herders are implacable and slow to anger, they are seen as headstrong and impatient by the ancient Forest Wardens. To provoke these massive woodland guardians to war is both an impressive feat and a dire mistake, for once angered they are nigh-unstoppable foes.

Tree Herder
Hero (Mon)

Unit Size	Sp	Me	Ra	De	Att	Ne	Pts
1	6	3+	–	6+	7	18/20	260

Special

Crushing Strength (3), Inspiring, Surge (8), Vanguard

Possibly the longest-lived mortal beings of all of Mantica, the Tree Herders remember the days before the Elves, when the Celestians walked through the virgin forests of a primeval world unspoilt by war and grief. These benign creatures care deeply for the other dwellers of the forest, so when angered they make the most implacable of foes.

Centaur Chief
Hero (Cav)

Unit Size	Sp	Me	Ra	De	Att	Ne	Pts
1	8	3+	–	4+	4	11/13	105

Special

Crushing Strength (2), Thunderous Charge (1), Inspiring, Individual

Options

- Bow gaining Ra 4+ for +10pts
- Wild Companion (+10 pts)

Few among the Centaurs aspire to leadership or great deeds, but those who lead their herds are a breed apart. They have seen many battles and hardships, and their martial prowess has been tempered by long years in the service of the Green Lady.

Naiad Stalker — Hero (Inf)

Unit Size	Sp	Me	Ra	De	Att	Ne	Pts
1	6	3+	–	4+	4	11/13	90

Special
Crushing Strength (1), Individual,
Inspiring (Naiads only), Regeneration (4+), Stealthy

Options
• Harpoon-gun, gaining Ra 4+ and Piercing (1) for +20pts
• Wild Companion for +10 pts

Solitary figures among the capricious Naiads, these sea-spirits have sworn to avenge those sisters who have fallen to the predations of sailors and soldiers over the long centuries. Their bitterness and rage has coalesced into magical power that transforms them into spirits of vengeance.

Winged Unicorn — Hero (Lrg Cav)

Unit Size	Sp	Me	Ra	De	Att	Ne	Pts
1	10	3+	–	5+	4	12/14	170

Special
Fly, Heal (7), Inspiring, Thunderous Charge (2)

Options
• Lightning Bolt (5) for +20pts
• Wind Blast (5) for +20pts
• Bane-chant (2) for +15pts

Known as the monarchs of all Pegasi, Unicorns, Centaurs and horses, these majestic winged creatures are the rarest and most graceful creatures in Mantica. Though hunted almost to extinction, they risk all by answering the Green Lady's call in times of war.

Salamander Veteran — Hero (Inf)

Unit Size	Sp	Me	Ra	De	Att	Ne	Pts
1	5	3+	-	5+	4	11/13	85

Special
Base Size: 25x25mm, Crushing Strength (2),
Individual, Inspiring (Salamanders only)

Options
• Wild Companion for +10 pts

These powerful reptilian warriors have undergone the Ordeal of Fire, an ancient ritual that lends the champions strength and ferocity far in advance of their lesser kin.

Unicorn — Hero (Cav)

Unit Size	Sp	Me	Ra	De	Att	Ne	Pts
1	10	3+	–	5+	3	11/13	120

Special
Heal (5), Individual, Thunderous Charge (2)

Though many fables tell of fair maids who have ridden upon the backs of a majestic unicorns, it is long held that these horned horses cannot be tamed or broken. They are powerful allies of the Druids, fast, deadly, and capable of healing the most grievous wounds with but a glance.

Pegasus · Hero (Lrg Cav)

Unit Size	Sp	Me	Ra	De	Att	Ne	Pts
1	10	3+	–	4+	3	10/12	80

Special
Fly, Thunderous Charge (1)

Gentle creatures of the air, it is rare to see a Pegasus take to battle unless it has been subdued and harnessed by an aggressor. However, when the Green Lady's domain is threatened, these majestic beasts circle the battlefield, picking off isolated enemies and vulnerable war machines.

The Green Lady [1] · Hero (Inf)

Unit Size	Sp	Me	Ra	De	At	Ne	Pts
1	10	–	–	6+	–	14/16	200

Special
Elite, Fly, Heal (8), Individual, Inspiring, Regeneration (5+)

Options
• Up to 2 Wild Companions (+10pts each)

The Wild Guard
The Wild Guard are the most devoted guardians of the Green Lady, sworn to protect her and to uphold her ideals until death takes them.

If your army includes the Green Lady, for +20 points you may upgrade a single Regiment of Hunters of the Wild to represent the Green Lady's Wild Guard, her most devoted and sworn guardians. This unit has the Headstrong and Regeneration (5+) special rules.

A Celestian of ages past, given form as a being of the deep woods, the Green Lady is worshipped as a goddess by the Druid Order, who lend their great power to her armies. Manifesting as a ghostly maid, tall as an oak and swift as a falcon, the Lady oft uses her powers to heal her loyal subjects. Yet her beautiful form belies the terrible ferocity that lies barely skin deep, waiting to be unleashed...

Keris [1] · Hero (Inf)

Unit Size	Sp	Me	Ra	De	Att	Ne	Pts
1	5	4+	–	4+	1	12/14	160

Special
Fireball (7), Heal (1), Individual, Inspiring, Lightning Bolt (2), Solar Staff, Surge (8)

Options
• Can be accompanied by Ozzee (Wild Companion) for +10 pts

Solar staff
The bearer has a single ranged attack with a range of 24" that always hits on 4+ (regardless of modifiers). If the target unit is hit, it is blinded until the end of its following Shoot phase – place a suitable marker next to the target. As long as it's blinded, the unit cannot Charge and is Disordered.

Shaarlyot [1] · Hero (Inf)

Unit Size	Sp	Me	Ra	De	Att	Ne	Pts
1	10	4+	–	3+	1	12/14	150

Special
Fireball (10), Fly, Individual, Inspiring, Wind Blast (7)

Options
• Can be accompanied by Tiffee (Wild Companion) for +10 pts

Keris is a young, headstrong Druid initiate, and bearer of the Solar Staff; Shaarlyot is a princess of the Sylphs, a gifted air-shaper and creature of the skies. And yet, through adversity and opposition from both the Sylphs and the Druid Order, these two unlikely companions have found love. While their relationship has caused great consternation, none can doubt their staunch commitment to the defence of the Whychwell Forest against the Elves and Undead who would both seek to unbalance the natural order.

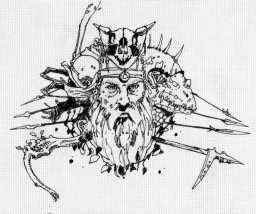

OGRE ARMIES

From their simple, nomadic camps in the far north of Mantica, where the frozen Mammoth Steppe rolls into untold miles of sweeping, barren grassland, a mere handful of Ogres descend each year; each embarking on a quest of fortune as is the age-old tradition for those who reach maturity. For sadly, a great many do not.

Reared in that harsh and unforgiving landscape of wild beasts, extreme temperatures and bandits of every imaginable variety, those Ogres that do survive the life or death trials of a childhood fraught with peril emerge as finely honed warriors indeed. They make for an arresting sight – with prominent jaws, barrel-sized fists and broad shoulders resembling a mountain-range of muscle, they stand taller and wider than any man and are renowned not only for their imposing size and brute strength but also their unwavering backbone. They fear no other being, and once an Ogre has set his sights there is little hope of preventing him from obtaining his prize. There is an expression among Dwarves that "an Ogre is always at its peak". Doubling as a pun on how they never leave their home-herd entirely unprotected, a gravely serious warning lies behind the humour of such phrases: that no matter its age, an Ogre is always dangerous if crossed.

The broad strokes of Ogre history are poorly recorded among their own kin, instead they hold with the tradition of passing down oft embellished tales of individual Ogres who have gone before - of their personal travels, exploits and adventures in the southern lands. These are never written down, and remain very personal, detailed and treasured tales, usually only circulated within a particular family or extended tribe. In fact, greater historical accuracy is found in the dusty books of the other races than among Ogres themselves. They have no head for it, no sense of territorial birth right or political purpose in the swirling landscape of constantly warring factions. They look on such things as endless, petty

Ogre Army Special Rules

Alignment: Neutral

Hammer Blow
All units in this list have the Brutal special rule, unless specified otherwise.

Note: Red Goblin units are not Brutal, but on the other hand neither are they 'Yellow Bellied' – it's the thought of what would happen to them if they disobeyed their Ogre masters.

squabbles with no real bearing on the existence of their remote people. As such, Ogres bear no ancient grudges, hold no inherent prejudice, and instead remain neutral, and when arriving for the first time at the gates of a city are very much open to all. Having usually heard exciting tales of such places from their elders, but being yet to personally experience the many and varied sensations on offer in such a place, their yearning appetites are enormous, and each is naturally endowed with a deep-seeded determination to boldly follow in the footsteps of their immediate forebears.

Despite their fearsome appearance and reputation, Ogres possess an often surprising sophistication of speech, an asset of any story-telling people, and one which has long allowed them to consort freely with the more civilised races they encounter on their travels. In this way, Ogres easily find employment and adventure in the south by offering their intimidating presence and combative prowess to the highest bidder. Having acquired a taste for it, they can easily become intoxicated by the praise and flattery afforded them, becoming vainglorious in the extreme and hugely desirous of ever more wealth and status, incessantly seeking to expedite their arrival at the heart of the

next battle, where fierce reputations can be forged and upheld. This in turn allows them to command higher and higher sums for their deadly services. As such, most quickly learn to value their own notoriety above all else, for nothing serves a mercenary better than his name preceding him, at least for the short duration of his southern odyssey. Between contracts, the more successful Ogres are able to bask in the heady excesses of gold and glory, before one day returning north, laden above all with tales to tell the next generation gathered at the campfire.

When Ogres do unite into larger war-parties with a common goal it is a rare thing indeed, and an Ogre army on the march is a sensory experience never to be forgotten: an ear-shattering clash of competing egos, with each determined to prove his superior ferocity or demonstrate his most spine-sundering battlecry. No unit will commit to battle as earnestly as an Ogre will, and they will fight to the very last, each straining to outdo the next until no enemy remains standing.

Wielding two-handed blades, heavy shields and immense blunderbusses the likes of which most men could not even hope to lift, an individual Ogre counts as many multiples of lesser troops when it comes to pure destructive force. Once into the fray, Ogres delight in using their astonishingly powerful limbs to grab, crush and literally cast aside any obstacle that stands between them and their goal, be it a hefty bounty or simply the prestige of having shattered more skulls than any other warrior in the field that day.

There is no record of an army ever holding fast against them, and scholars debate long into the night as to whether this is because Ogres have so rarely united in force, or because no opposition has ever survived tell the tale.

Warriors · Large Infantry

Unit Size	Sp	Me	Ra	De	Att	Ne	Pts
Regiment (3)	6	3+	–	5+	9	12/14	130
Horde (6)	6	3+	–	5+	18	15/17	200
Legion (12)	6	3+	–	5+	36	22/24	350

Special

Crushing Strength (1)

Options

• Exchange shields with two-handed weapons for free (lower Defence to 4+, but gain Crushing Strength (2))

Hulking, massively muscled creatures, Ogre warriors are twice the height of a man, and many times his weight.

Berserker Braves · Large Infantry

Unit Size	Sp	Me	Ra	De	Att	Ne	Pts
Regiment (3)	6	4+	–	4+	15	-/15	150
Horde (6)	6	4+	–	4+	30	-/18	230

Special

Crushing Strength (1)

These chosen few become a Warlock's followers – a devoted, close-knit group of fanatical neophytes. All are trained in Ogre lore, devotion to the Ogre gods and, for those with the gift, training in the spiritual and mental conditioning required of a future tribal Shaman.

Siege Breakers · Large Infantry

Unit Size	Sp	Me	Ra	De	Att	Ne	Pts
Regiment (3)	5	3+	–	4+	9	12/14	165
Horde (6)	5	3+	–	4+	18	15/17	250

Special

Big Shield, Crushing Strength (3), Thunderous Charge (1)

Ogres specialising in breaking down castle gates, they carry huge mallets and wear very heavy armour.

Hunters · Large Infantry

Unit Size	Sp	Me	Ra	De	Att	Ne	Pts
Regiment (3)	6	3+	–	4+	9	12/14	145
Horde (6)	6	3+	–	4+	18	15/17	220

Special

Crushing Strength (1), Ensnare, Pathfinder

Bands of hunters equipped with small tree trunks they use as hunting spears, heavy nets and a plethora of axes, skinning knives (large, large knives...), etc.

Shooters — Large Infantry

Unit Size	Sp	Me	Ra	De	Att	Ne	Pts
Regiment (3)	6	4+	5+	4+	9	12/14	150
Horde (6)	6	4+	5+	4+	18	15/17	230

Special

Heavy crossbows, Crushing Strength (1), Piercing (2), Reload!

Ogre Shooters carry large crossbows the size of small ballistae.

Boomers — Large Infantry

Unit Size	Sp	Me	Ra	De	Att	Ne	Pts
Regiment (3)	6	4+	-	4+	9	12/14	150
Horde (6)	6	4+	-	4+	18	15/17	230

Special

Breath Attack (Att), Crushing Strength (1), Piercing (1)

Ogres Boomers carry fearsome blunderbusses that are more akin to short-ranged cannon than any firearm a man might wield.

Chariots — Large Cavalry

Unit Size	Sp	Me	Ra	De	Att	Ne	Pts
Regiment (3)	7	3+	–	5+	12	12/14	170
Horde (6)	7	3+	–	5+	24	15/17	265

Special

Base Size: 50x100mm, Crushing Strength (1), Thunderous Charge (2)

Organised in thundering squadrons, these very heavy chariots are easily capable of shattering the most organised of battlelines.

Red Goblins * — Infantry

Unit Size	Sp	Me	Ra	De	Att	Ne	Pts
Regiment (20)	5	6+	5+	3+	10	12/14	85
Horde (40)	5	6+	5+	3+	20	19/21	140

Special

Bows

Many Goblins and other lesser creatures are attracted to the wealth and power of Ogre mercenary armies. They become camp followers and attend to all of the most menial of tasks in an Ogre encampment, but are occasionally used as support archers by the Ogres, who have noticed the little ones' ability with the bow.

Traditionally the Ogres request 'their' Goblins to wear red rags in order to distinguish them from the enemy in the mayhem of battle, thus avoiding unpleasant incidents. This has led to the nickname of 'Red Goblins', that these creature bear now with great pride.

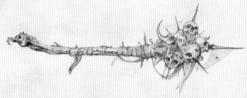

Red Goblin Scouts * — Cavalry

Unit Size	Sp	Me	Ra	De	Att	Ne	Pts
Troop (5)	10	4+	-	4+	7	9/11	100
Regiment (10)	10	4+	-	4+	14	12/14	155

Special

Thunderous Charge (1), Nimble

Fleabags flock naturally to groups of Goblins, even more so where they can feed on the tasty scraps of the Ogre's leftover food. Packs of Red Goblins mounted on the largest Fleabags make perfect scouts and sentries for Ogre armies on the move.

Red Goblin Blaster Monster

Unit Size	Sp	Me	Ra	De	Att	Ne	Pts
1	5	–	–	5+	*	8/10	65

Special

Base Size: 50x100mm, Height 3

The Red Goblin operator (whose model, by the way, is always ignored) can trigger the Blaster explosion at any point during any of its Shoot phases, even if it has moved At The Double or is Disordered that turn – all units (friend and foe) within D6" of the Blaster model suffer 2D6 hits with Piercing (4), and then the Blaster model is immediately Routed. Roll the number of hits once, but then roll to damage individually for each unit hit. Friendly units taking damage as a result do not have to take Nerve tests, but enemy units will do as normal.

If a Blaster routs as a result of a Nerve test, it explodes as above.

*If a Blaster charges an enemy unit, it will simply detonate in the Shoot phase as above.

The most common tactic for this weapon is to charge an enemy unit or, even better, run it as close as possible to the enemy and then trigger the explosion. It often works...

Mammoth Monster

Unit Size	Sp	Me	Ra	De	Att	Ne	Pts
1	7	4+	–	5+	12	15/17	210

Special

Base Size: 50x100mm, Crushing Strength (2), Thunderous Charge (2)

Options

• Mount a Ballista on it: Range 36", Ra 5+, 2 Ranged Attacks, Blast (D3), Piercing (2) for +10 pts

Great beasts of the Steppe, herded or even ridden to war by Ogre chieftains.

Giant Monster

Unit Size	Sp	Me	Ra	De	Att	Ne	Pts
1	7	4+	–	5+	(D6+6)*	17/19	190

Special

Fury, Crushing Strength (3), Strider

* Roll for the number of Attacks every time you resolve a melee

A Giant is a huge humanoid, a veritable mountain of bone, sinew and flesh with a very, very tiny brain and a massive appetite.

Warlord — Hero (Lrg Inf)

Unit Size	Sp	Me	Ra	De	Att	Ne	Pts
1	6	3+	–	5+	7	15/17	175

Special

Crushing Strength (2), Inspiring, Nimble

Options

- Exchange shield with two-handed weapon for free (lower Defence to 4+, but gain Crushing Strength (3)).
- Mount on chariot for +15 pts, gaining Thunderous Charge (2) and Speed 7, but losing Nimble and changing to Hero (Large Cav) on a 50x100mm base.

Sometimes, the Ogres march to war en masse; to face great threats to their lands or to search out new hunting grounds. When this occurs, mighty Ogre Warlords lead their tribes to total war – survival or death!

Captain — Hero (Lrg Inf)

Unit Size	Sp	Me	Ra	De	Att	Ne	Pts
1	6	3+	5+	5+	5	13/15	135

Special

Crushing Strength (2), Inspiring, Nimble

Options

- Exchange shield with two-handed weapon for free (lower Defence to 4+, but gain Crushing Strength (3)).
- Exchange shield with heavy crossbow (gain Reload! and Piercing (2), but lower Defence to 4+), for +10pts.
- Mount on chariot for +15 pts, gaining Thunderous Charge (2) and Speed 7, but losing Nimble and changing to Hero (Large Cav) on a 50x100mm base.

Ogre captains are among the mightiest of this race of war-loving veterans.

Army Standard — Hero (Lrg Inf)

Unit Size	Sp	Me	Ra	De	Att	Ne	Pts
1	6	3+	–	4+	3	11/13	70

Special

Crushing Strength (1), Inspiring, Nimble

Options

- Mount on chariot for +15 pts (gain Thunderous Charge (2), Defence 5+ and Speed 7, but losing Nimble) and changing to Hero (Large Cav) on a 50x100mm base.

Wily Ogre Captains nominate trusted Sergeants to take responsibility for the best of the band's treasures, proudly displaying them in times of war to rally the troops and make them yearn for more.

Warlock — Hero (Lrg Inf)

Unit Size	Sp	Me	Ra	De	Att	Ne	Pts
1	6	4+	–	4+	2	12/14	100

Special

Crushing Strength (1), Inspiring (Berserker Braves only), Lightning Bolt (3), Nimble.

In addition, the Warlock gains an additional dice for spells for each unit of Berserker Braves within 6".

Options

Fireball (12) for +30pts

Wind Blast (5) for +30pts

Ogre Warlocks are revered amongst the tribes of the Steppe and often fulfil the roles of shaman, witch-doctor and spiritual guide within the nomadic communities. On the battlefield, Ogre Warlocks are often accompanied by their devoted and fanatical pupils and followers.

Boomer Sergeant — Hero (Lrg Inf)

Unit Size	Sp	Me	Ra	De	Att	Ne	Pts
1	6	4+	–	4+	4	11/13	90

Special

Breath Attack (Att), Crushing Strength (1), Nimble, Piercing (1)

Ogres are a surprisingly disciplined race, which in conjunction with their enormous size and strength has contributed to their success as mercenaries. A Boomer Sergeant can always be confident that the warriors under him will do exactly as ordered. Carrying a weapon with the size, weight and power of small cannon helps as well.

Siege Master

Hero (Lrg Inf)

Unit Size	Sp	Me	Ra	De	Att	Ne	Pts
1	5	3+	–	4+	4	12/14	135

Special

Big Shield, Crushing Strength (3), Inspiring (Siege Breakers only), Nimble, Thunderous Charge (1)

To get through any fortress gate, accept no substitute.

Red Goblin Biggit

Hero (Inf)

Unit Size	Sp	Me	Ra	De	Att	Ne	Pts
1	5	4+	4+	4+	3	9/11	60

Special

Bow, Individual, Inspiring (Red Goblin units only)

Options

• Mount on a Fleabag, increasing Speed to 10 (+15 pts and changing to Hero (Cav)

Goblins are often to be found fighting alongside Ogre bands, attracted by the lure of wealth and power, as well as the respect that Ogres command. Inevitably, some of the iron hard discipline and fighting creeds of the Ogres will wear off on the Gobbos over time, and the Biggits are those who best imitate their oversized comrades, taking charge of their kin and directing them on the field.

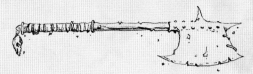

Grokagamok [1]

Hero (Lrg Inf)

Unit Size	Sp	Me	Ra	De	Att	Ne	Pts
1	6	3+	–	5+	7	15/17	260

Special

The Amputator, Crushing Strength (3), Nimble, Very Inspiring

The Amputator

The bearer of this massive axe has an increased Crushing Strength (already included in the profile).

In addition, the bearer's Melee attacks also have the Blast (D3) special rule.

Leader of the infamous Granite Fists mercenary company, Grokagamok is undoubtedly the most renowned and successful Ogre mercenary captain in the world. Though he prefers to work with humans (they tend to be happier to pay and more likely to stay out of the way and let him and his troops get on with it), he has worked with most races at some point or other. Like his kin, as long as there is pay in it, he will accept any job, and this attitude, combined with the skill of him and the Granite Fists, has seen them become wealthier than several small nations.

FORCES OF THE ABYSS

The Abyss lies many leagues north-east of Basilea, and yet for many it is still too close for comfort, for it is the home of all that is evil in Mantica. Around the outer edges of the Abyss have grown many evil civilisations, corrupted by the dark influence that leaks from within. The empires of the Twilight Kin and Abyssal Dwarves as well as countless Orcs, Goblins and other wretched creatures all exist there. Further down this hellish crevasse, the taint of the malevolent energies of the Wicked Ones becomes stronger, and things far worse than Orcs dwell.

Forces of the Abyss Special Rules

Alignment: Evil

Abyssal Vengeance
All units in this list have Fury, unless specified otherwise.

The Abyss is a chasm, both literal and metaphorical, in the skin of the world. It is thought by many to be a vast, physical cleft in the earth, leading to some cyclopean, volcanic depth far below. This is only partly true, for mortals must ever reconcile that which they cannot understand with absolutes. The deeper one ventures into this dizzying realm of darkness, the more it becomes obvious that the Abyss and all its denizens are anathema to natural law.

The veil between planes of existence is thin, a dark parody of the power of the old Celestians to walk between worlds. Bare rock breathes with bilious life; black smoke coils with dark sentience, corrupting all that breathe it; measureless caverns convulse and twist into labyrinths that would take a lifetime to traverse. Countless tortured souls gibber as they suffer exquisite pain in the endless dark, their fevered imaginings giving form to new realities, new monstrosities, and new sorceries. Deep down in the shadows and billowing fumes, perpetually lit by the glow of hellish red fires, fouler creatures reside – beings of unfettered evil, whose very existence is an abomination against the natural order of things, living in a twisted mirror of the celestial orders above.

These are the Abyssals, immortal servants of the Father of Lies. The Abyssals are emanations of their Lord's mind – pure Evil incarnated. They are organized into a strict hierarchy, which perversely mirrors that

of the celestial hosts of the Shining Ones, and is related to which level, or 'circle' of the Abyss in which they reside. Ruling over this hierarchy are the supreme beings that dwell in the depths of the Seventh Circle, which is at the very bottom of the Abyss – they are the twenty-seven Wicked Ones, brethren of the Father of Lies, bound by the power of Domivar never to leave the Abyss, and yet ever plotting and scheming to exert their will onto the mortal realm. It is said that the Wicked Ones live in the Eternal Dark, inimical to life both mortal and Abyssal, and yet these godlike beings endure, their power manifest in every corner of their realm.

The will of the Wicked Ones is interpreted and enacted by the most powerful of their servants – the Archfiends, Lords of the Sixth Circle, who are the generals of the Abyssal host, creatures of great might, both physical and sorcerous. The Sixth Circle has never been seen by mortal eyes, and if it were it would surely drive them to madness. In these cursed depths, impossible towers of brimstone and gleaming crystal twist into endless skies of fire and blood. Atop monuments made from the remains of vanquished foes sit

effigies of nameless gods from forgotten planes, at their feet lumbering Molochs train endlessly for war in brutal testing grounds. As opposed to the Wicked Ones, the foul Archfiends can leave the Abyss when the signs are right, and will march at the head of their legions to unleash the Power of the Abyss upon the world.

Beyond these dominating planes, the story is much the same. Each Circle of the Abyss increases in size to accommodate the burgeoning hordes that dwell there, and yet diminishes in power the farther from the sight of the Wicked Ones they are cast.

The Fifth Circle is the abode of the Abyssal Champions, crafty lower Abyssals that have gained the favour of the Wicked Ones and been elevated to levels of power beyond what most of their kind can imagine. These Champions draw countless slaves from the lesser circles to construct mighty fortresses and monuments to their strength, exerting cruel power over their one-time brethren. It is not unknown for a Champion to rise as a mighty conqueror, bloated with power, and to take to the mortal world at the head of his own army.

The Fourth Circle is a plane of fire, which feeds the volcanic pits that mark the bounds between the Dark and the mortal realm. Here, the blessed children of Ariagful walk upon conflagrating seas, seeking egress into the world beyond. It is a realm ruled over by the demonic Efreets, who oversee the forging of great artefacts for the armies of the Archfiends.

The Third Circle is a wellspring of magic and corruption that feeds the other circles, above and below. Here, Succubi and Temptresses practice perverse sorceries on victims plucked from the mortal realm, while lumbering Chroneas manipulate time itself so that the tortured souls can experience their torment for all eternity.

The Second Circle is a wild land, a blasted waste inhabited by bestial creatures of raw strength and rage. Across plains of ash, hordes of nomadic horsemen engage in the

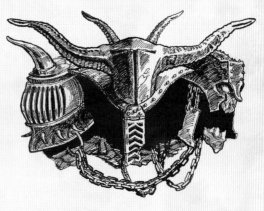

endless hunt. Once mortal, these creatures are now corrupted beyond recognition, and ride down the tortured souls of the Abyss for sport.

The bulk of the Abyssal denizens are born of the First Circle, which straddles both the mortal realm and the incorporeal domains below. Here, in seemingly limitless numbers, Lower Abyssals and winged Gargoyles are birthed from volcanic pits, breathing in toxic miasma as if it were clean air. These sly, cruel creatures are usually to be found tending to the torture of mortals who have been dragged back to the Abyss, but fight for supremacy amongst themselves constantly, so that when they are summoned to war they have already been tempered by battle. Tiny Imps scamper through black caverns, serving the more powerful Abyssal Warriors as a means to survive, or else ending up as prey for the many predators that lurk in the darkness.

At the signal from the Archfiends, great shadow-bridges are formed between the circles, and the Molochs adopt the role of enforcers, herding the Abyssals together into a mighty demonic horde. Plumes of ash and coruscating arcs of pure magic erupt from the heart of the Abyss. War-horns sound, and the ground trembles as the armies of the Wicked Ones begin their march of conquest. When these creatures venture forth from the pit, they spread like a stain across the surface of the world. Crops wither and die under their tread, and their shadow blights the world until they are banished back to the Dark whence they came, but always at great cost.

Abyssal Guard
Infantry

Unit Size	Sp	Me	Ra	De	Att	Ne	Pts
Troop (10)	5	3+	–	5+	10	11/13	110
Regiment (20)	5	3+	–	5+	12	15/17	160

Special
Regeneration (5+)

Options
• Exchange shields for two-handed weapons for free (lower Defence to 4+, gain Crushing Strength (1))

The existence of a Lower Abyssal is one governed by constant violence and bloodshed, even amongst themselves. Those who rise to the top of the pile, by dint of cunning, martial prowess or most likely a combination of the two, will earn the right to don ceremonial armour and wield more powerful weapons.

Larvae*
Infantry

Unit Size	Sp	Me	Ra	De	Att	Ne	Pts
Horde (40)	5	6+	–	4+	25	-/22	130
Legion (60)	5	6+	–	4+	30	-/28	190

Special
Ensnare, Shambling

Those tortured mortals who have lost all trace of cognisance and sanity are often bundled together into a mass of wailing soul-vessels, terrible to behold. They are driven forward by their Abyssal torturers with pitch-forks and barbed whips, demonstrating beyond doubt that to face the Abyss is to lose all hope.

Flamebearers
Infantry

Unit Size	Sp	Me	Ra	De	Att	Ne	Pts
Troop (10)	5	5+	4+	3+	8	10/12	105
Regiment (20)	5	5+	4+	3+	10	14/16	140

Special
Firebolts, Piercing (1), Regeneration (5+)

These lesser Abyssals are pressed into service of the Efreet. Imbued with fire magic, they cast bolts of flaming energy at their foes, searing the battlefield with sorcerous fire.

Lower Abyssals — Infantry

Unit Size	Sp	Me	Ra	De	Att	Ne	Pts
Troop (10)	5	4+	–	4+	10	10/12	85
Regiment (20)	5	4+	–	4+	12	14/16	120
Horde (40)	5	4+	–	4+	25	21/23	200

Special
Regeneration (5+)

Options
• Exchange shields for two-handed weapons for free (lower Defence to 3+, gain Crushing Strength (1))

Given life by the energies of the most dark and powerful magic, these semi-corporeal creatures take on the shape of the worst nightmares of mortal races. Red skinned and vicious, they are capable fighters who slay their foes with wicked blades and flaming attacks.

Gargoyles * — Infantry

Unit Size	Sp	Me	Ra	De	Att	Ne	Pts
Troop (10)	10	4+	–	3+	8	9/11	80

Special
Base Sizes: 25x25mm, Fly, Regeneration (3+), Vicious
Note: this unit does not have the Fury special rule.

These lesser Abyssals of limited intelligence follow the armies of their evil kin, darkening the skies like a sinister pall, ready to plunge on the wounded and the stragglers with voracious appetite.

Succubi — Infantry

Unit Size	Sp	Me	Ra	De	Att	Ne	Pts
Troop (10)	6	3+	–	3+	20	10/12	135
Regiment (20)	6	3+	–	3+	25	14/16	190

Special
Ensnare, Stealthy.

The embodiment of a mortal's basest desires, Succubi are torturers and tormentors, who use their seductive appearance to lull their enemies into submission, drawing them close before tearing them limb from limb with their razor-sharp blades.

Fleshlings — Infantry

Unit Size	Sp	Me	Ra	De	Att	Ne	Pts
Troop (10)	5	5+	–	4+	10	10/12	65
Regiment (20)	5	5+	–	4+	12	14/16	90
Horde (40)	5	5+	–	4+	25	21/23	150

Options
• Exchange shields for two-handed weapons for free (lower Defence to 3+, gain Crushing Strength (1))

There are some mortals for whom the lure of the Abyss is too great. Men, Elves and Dwarfs often make their way to the great chasm, setting up camp on its outskirts and worshipping the dark denizens below. Becoming ever more twisted and corrupt, they follow the Abyssal legions to war in great, ragtag mobs.

Hellhounds   Cavalry

Unit Size	Sp	Me	Ra	De	Att	Ne	Pts
Troop (5)	9	4+	–	4+	15	10/12	125

Special

Height 1, Nimble, Thunderous Charge (1)

A Hellhound is a vicious beast with three demonic heads and snapping jaws full of enormous teeth. Used as hunting dogs by the denizens of the Abyss, these terrifying beasts are as ferocious as they are ugly and unpredictable – prone to attack anything within reach, friend or foe.

Imps*   Large Infantry

Unit Size	Sp	Me	Ra	De	Att	Ne	Pts
Regiment (3)	5	5+	–	3+	12	11/13	70
Horde (6)	5	5+	–	3+	24	14/16	105

Special

Height 0, Vicious

These diminutive Homunculi are found on every level of the Abyss, whether as servants, pets, torturers or tasty delicacies. They are chittering, spiteful, vicious little monsters, as like to slit a warrior's throat as to play a childish prank on him.

Abyssal Horsemen   Cavalry

Unit Size	Sp	Me	Ra	De	Att	Ne	Pts
Troop (5)	8	3+	–	5+	9	11/13	140
Regiment (10)	8	3+	–	5+	18	14/16	215

Special

Crushing Strength (1), Thunderous Charge (1)

These mysterious, heavily armoured riders are often armed with lances or huge, two-handed weapons. It is said that they were once mortal, and yet were elevated to the service of the Wicked Ones. It is tales such as these that prove a persistent lure to mortals who lust after power at any cost.

Tortured Souls   Large Infantry

Unit Size	Sp	Me	Ra	De	Att	Ne	Pts
Regiment (3)	10	4+	–	4+	9	–/15	145
Horde (6)	10	4+	–	4+	18	–/18	220

Special

Crushing Strength (2), Fly, Lifeleech (2), Shambling

The degenerates known as 'Tortured Souls' are those adventurers who thought themselves strong enough to defy the lure of the Abyss. Stripped of all identity, they are little more than beasts, driven by the instinctive desire to drain the souls of the living, in the hope that they might free themselves from their eternal torment.

Molochs
Large Infantry

Unit Size	Sp	Me	Ra	De	Att	Ne	Pts
Regiment (3)	5	4+	–	4+	12	12/15	130
Horde (6)	5	4+	–	4+	24	15/18	200

Special
Base Size: 50x50mm, Crushing Strength (2), Brutal

Huge, lumbering beasts, and more powerful cousins to the Lower Abyssals, Molochs tend to be solitary creatures, for their rage can barely be contained. Occasionally they band together into small groups when war calls, but these pacts never last for long before another bout of infighting breaks out.

Chroneas
Monster

Unit Size	Sp	Me	Ra	De	Att	Ne	Pts
1	5	-	–	5+	-	16/18	210

Special
Breath Attack (20), Pathfinder, Piercing (1), Tempus (this unit cannot be Disordered)

It is said that these black-skinned beasts have roamed the world since its creation, and only after the Sundering found service in the legions of the Wicked Ones. Around them, time can flow faster or more slowly than elsewhere, and their enemies are often caused to wither and die in a heartbeat as the curse of ages is placed upon them.

Abyssal Champion — Hero (Inf)

Unit Size	Sp	Me	Ra	De	Att	Ne	Pts
1	5	3+	–	5+	5	13/15	135

Special

Crushing Strength (1), Individual, Inspiring, Regeneration (5+).

Options

• Can have wings for +40 pts (gaining Fly and increasing Speed to 10)
• Lightning Bolt (5), for +40pts
• Can ride an abyssal mount, increasing Speed to 8, for +20 pts and changing to Hero (Cav)

An Abyssal Champion is a Lower Abyssal that has distinguished itself under the watchful gaze of the Archfiends (or, rarely, of the Lords of the Abyss themselves). Rewarded with powers far superior to his dark kin, the creature has now become a leader amongst them: an example to follow and a cruel master to be obeyed.

Abyssal Temptress — Hero (Inf)

Unit Size	Sp	Me	Ra	De	Att	Ne	Pts
1	6	3+	–	4+	5	11/13	90

Special

Ensnare, Individual, Inspiring (Succubi only), Stealthy

Options

• Bane Chant (2) for +15 pts
• Wind Blast (6) for +30 pts
• Can have wings for +30 pts (gaining Fly and increasing Speed to 10)

The matriarchs of the Succubi orders, Temptresses oversee the eternal torture and delicious pain of the most prized captives in the Abyss. In battle, they can appear as beautiful maids, irresistible to all, and yet in an instant become a fanged harridan bringing swift death to their foes.

Efreet — Hero (Inf)

Unit Size	Sp	Me	Ra	De	Att	Ne	Pts
1	7	4+	–	4+	1	11/13	135

Special

Fireball (20), Individual, Pathfinder

Moulded by the furnaces of the infernal pit, Efreets are suffused in flickering, magical flames. They propel themselves forwards on a column of fire, and shoot fireballs from their clawed fists, which burn hot enough to melt armour and turn bones to ash in the blink of an eye.

Abyssal Harbinger — Hero (Inf)

Unit Size	Sp	Me	Ra	De	Att	Ne	Pts
1	5	5+	4+	4+	1	10/12	60

Special

Firebolt, Individual, Inspiring, Piercing (1), Regeneration (5+).

Options

• Can ride an abyssal mount, increasing Speed to 8, for +15 pts and changing to Hero (Cav)

For many Lower Abyssals, life in the Abyss is violent and short, with no chance to attain the favour of their masters. There are some, however, possessed of more ambition than to merely accept their lot. These creatures sometimes strike unholy alliances with the lesser beasts of the First Circle, fusing with their mount to create an altogether new, and utterly freakish, abomination.

Archfiend of the Abyss — Hero (Mon)

Unit Size	Sp	Me	Ra	De	Att	Ne	Pts
1	7	3+	–	5+	9	16/18	250

Special

Brutal, Crushing Strength (2), Inspiring, Thunderous Charge (2), Vicious

Options

• Can have wings, gaining Fly and increasing Speed to 10 for +50 pts
• Lightning Bolt (5), for +25pts

Favoured of the Wicked Ones and generals supreme of the Abyssal legions, the Archfiends are the only denizens of the Abyss able to commune directly with their dark overlords. Creatures of great power, these towering Abyssals take many forms, from bloated, hellish behemoths to winged monstrosities.

Ba'su'su the Vile [1]   Hero (Inf)

Unit Size	Sp	Me	Ra	De	Att	Ne	Pts
1	10	3+	–	5+	8	15/17	220

Special

Base Size: 25x25mm, Crushing Strength (2), Fly, Individual, Inspiring (Gargoyles only), Regeneration (5+), Vicious

Vile Spawn

If your army includes Ba'su'su, for +20 pts you may upgrade a single unit of Gargoyles to represent his flock of elder Gargoyles. This unit has Defence 4+ and Crushing Strength (1).

A halfbreed of great power, Ba'su'su the Vile, Lord of Gargoyles, is a mighty pinioned monster, tormented by the low status his halfbreed nature condemns him to.

The Lord of Lies [1]   Hero (Lrg Inf)

Unit Size	Sp	Me	Ra	De	Att	Ne	Pts
1	10	3+	–	5+	5	15/20	300

Special

Crushing Strength (2), Ensnare, Fly, Inspiring, Lightning Bolt (7), Stealthy, Thunderous Charge (2)

The most devious of Archfiends, many believe this infernal creature is an avatar of Oskan himself; a limited means for the Father of Lies to escape the Eternal Dark. Many an opposing army has ended up tearing itself to pieces when faced with the subtle, manipulative powers of this most devious of fiends.

The Well of Souls [1]   Hero (Mon)

Unit Size	Sp	Me	Ra	De	Att	Ne	Pts
1	10	4+	–	5+	10	-/20	275

Special

Crushing Strength (2), Fly, Inspiring, Lifeleech (5), Shambling, Soul Drain

Soul Drain

The Well of Souls pulls the life force from the enemy and feeds the Abyssal army. When the Well of Souls is given an order, it may take up to 20 points of damage on itself. However, this cannot take it to more than 20 damage in total. For each point of damage taken in this way, it may remove one point of damage from a friendly non-Allied unit within 9". The Well of Souls will not take a nerve test for damage taken in this way.

The screaming void at the heart of the Abyss given form, it is hard to tell if the Well of Souls is sentient or merely a force of destruction. It tears across the battlefield as a screaming vortex, ripping the very souls from mortal foes and sucking them into the Abyss.

ABYSSAL DWARFS

The Abyss is not merely a physical rent in the earth, but a literal tear in reality itself. Populated by creatures of nightmare, brought into being by the will of the Wicked Ones who are exiled there, it is a place steeped in evil so powerful it is like a palpable thing. That evil works on the hearts and minds of any mortal who spends too long in proximity to it, worming its way in to find their weaknesses and amplifying them to twist the individual into something entirely different.

Thus it was with the unfortunate Dwarfs of the northern clans who established mining communities in the vicinity of the Abyss itself, north of the Halpi Mountains. Digging deep into the earth, they were exposed to this corrupting influence for decades, gradually corrupting their natural love of gold and other treasures. The noble attitudes of their people – the importance of honest sweat and toil and the earning of wealth – were slowly eroded, replaced by the all-consuming lust for ever more.

Abyssal Dwarfs Special Rules

Alignment: Evil

Cruel Masters
All units in this list have the Vicious special rule, unless specified otherwise.

Mutated Throwing Mastiffs
The Abyssal Dwarfs engage in wicked (but admittedly quite amusing) alchemically-adjusted cross-breeding of the traditional Dwarven Throwing Mastiff with all sorts of monstrous creatures.

Mutated Throwing Mastiffs are the same as Dwarven Throwing Mastiffs, except they re-roll failed rolls to damage against all enemies.

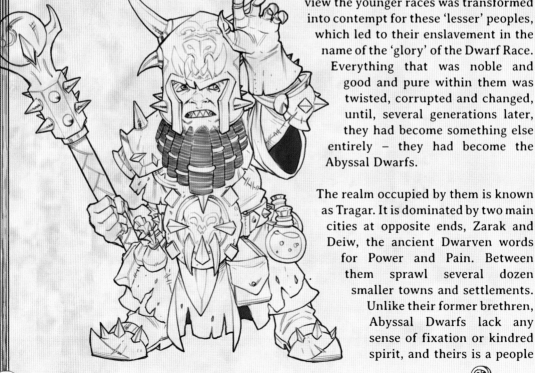

They began to dabble with sorcery to ease the burden of their labours. The natural disdain and suspicion with which Dwarfs view the younger races was transformed into contempt for these 'lesser' peoples, which led to their enslavement in the name of the 'glory' of the Dwarf Race. Everything that was noble and good and pure within them was twisted, corrupted and changed, until, several generations later, they had become something else entirely – they had become the Abyssal Dwarfs.

The realm occupied by them is known as Tragar. It is dominated by two main cities at opposite ends, Zarak and Deiw, the ancient Dwarven words for Power and Pain. Between them sprawl several dozen smaller towns and settlements. Unlike their former brethren, Abyssal Dwarfs lack any sense of fixation or kindred spirit, and theirs is a people

riven by internal politicking and strife. New clans, towns and even cities rise and fall in the space of decades as particular personalities rise to the top of the mire that is their society, and these often vie with one another for dominance.

Their obsession with sorcery has bitten deep into them, and the most powerful among them tend to be their Iron Casters. Often experimenting on slaves, their own kin and even themselves in their obsessive drive towards what they see as the perfection of the physical form, these twisted individuals combine the natural talent of the Dwarf for the mechanical with a deep and unnatural understanding of the sorcerous arts. It is no coincidence that the most powerful armies of the Abyssal Dwarfs are commanded by these individuals.

The Abyssal Dwarf

In physical appearance, these hateful creatures are basically similar to their kin. They are short and squat, powerfully built with thick yet dextrous fingers. But a second glance reveals many differences.

Paler of skin and lacking the ruddiness of complexion of the Dwarfs, Abyssal Dwarfs also tend more towards fat, their slovenly ways and reliance on slaves making them more portly. Their dress is also different, favouring elaborate goldwork and filigreeing in their helmets and armour, designed to emphasise their wealth and therefore their worth. The flinty, intelligent eyes of their cousins are replaced with dark gimlets which stare out at the world with undisguised loathing, and their faces are twisted into sneering masks.

One small blessing for the world at large is that the Abyssal Dwarfs seem slow to reproduce. Indeed, some theories abound that new Abyssal Dwarfs are never born, due to the unnatural energies surrounding the Abyss and their effect on the physical form. These people think that new Abyssal Dwarfs are simply created from Dwarfs who even now make the mistake of venturing too closely to Tragar. Others believe that Abyssal Dwarfs cannot die, and live eternally, thereby removing the need to spawn. Whatever the truth, it is a fact that any Abyssal Dwarf army will see the

Abyssal Dwarfs within it outnumbered by the slaves that they drive before them and the magical constructs they conjure to fight alongside them, sometime greatly so.

Their unhealthy obsession with sorcery and alchemical engineering has led to some of the most evil creations being spawned by the Abyssal Dwarfs. The so-called 'halfbreeds' – fusions of Abyssal Dwarfs with magical creatures – are terrifyingly powerful whilst also being utterly insane. Their weapons and machines are all powered as much by dark magic as they are by mechanical genius, and they know no boundaries or shame in the levels to which they will sink in the pursuit of power.

Their society operates on the basis of individual greed and lust for wealth, explaining its fluid and ever-changing nature, as various individuals rise to prominence, dominating their fellows and expanding their own tiny spaces into minor empires within Tragar before they topple once more. Only the twin cities

endure, built into the very bedrock of the mountains surrounding the Abyss and delving deep into it. Though the cities themselves flourish and thrive, their rulership is in a state of constant flux, with various powerful individuals making and breaking alliances as they all vie for rightful rulership of their people.

Occasionally, a leader will rise of such power and magnificence that he is able to unite the Abyssal Dwarfs as a race, and they will march forth to make war on the other civilised peoples of the world, driving their armies of slaves before them and supported by magical constructs and wicked creatures of darkness. These are dark times indeed, though thankfully short lived. The very fractious nature of the Abyssal Dwarf people tends to ensure that any alliance lasts only as long as it takes for the ambitions of another to arise. It is reason to be thankful, for should they ever unite on any permanent basis, it is without doubt that these foul beings could overrun the world and all those who live in it.

Blacksouls Infantry

Unit Size	Sp	Me	Ra	De	Att	Ne	Pts
Troop (10)	4	4+	–	5+	10	10/12	80
Regiment (20)	4	4+	–	5+	12	14/16	115
Horde (40)	4	4+	–	5+	25	21/23	190

Options
• Mutated Throwing Mastiff (+15 pts)

• Exchange shields for two-handed weapons for free
(lower Defence to 4+, gain Crushing Strength (1))

Advancing in tight ranks, clad in ancient Dwarf armour and protected by the dark powers of the Abyss, the Blacksouls are feared by all, and they never pass on a chance to add to the tally of misery and slaughter they are responsible for.

Abyssal Berserkers Infantry

Unit Size	Sp	Me	Ra	De	Att	Ne	Pts
Troop (10)	5	4+	–	3+	20	-/13	125
Regiment (20)	5	4+	–	3+	25	-/17	180

Special
Crushing Strength (1)

Dwarf Berserkers are easily swayed by the Abyss, convinced to give up their soul in return for the promise of eternal slaughter and a never-ending supply of willing foes.

Immortal Guard Infantry

Unit Size	Sp	Me	Ra	De	Att	Ne	Pts
Troop (10)	4	3+	–	5+	10	-/13	100
Regiment (20)	4	3+	–	5+	12	-/17	145

Options
• Mutated Throwing Mastiff (+15 pts)

• Exchange shields for two-handed weapons for free
(lower Defence to 4+, gain Crushing Strength (1))

The warriors forming the bodyguard of the Overmasters and Iron-casters are given the gift of eternal life. There is however a terrible price to pay for this 'honour', and many of these veterans end up as nothing more than war-thirsty spirits trapped inside ancient sets of fully enclosing armour.

Decimators Infantry

Unit Size	Sp	Me	Ra	De	Att	Ne	Pts
Troop (10)	4	5+	–	4+	10	10/12	120
Regiment (20)	4	5+	–	4+	12	14/16	160
Horde (40)	4	5+	–	4+	25	21/23	255

Special
Breath Attack (Att), Piercing (1)

The Decimators' weapons are cruder in construction when compared with the rifles of the Dwarfs, but what they lose in range and stopping power, they more than make up with close-range devastation.

Slave Orcs * Infantry

Unit Size	Sp	Me	Ra	De	Att	Ne	Pts
Troop (10)	5	4+	–	4+	10	9/11	65
Regiment (20)	5	4+	–	4+	12	13/15	90
Horde (40)	5	4+	–	4+	25	20/22	150

Special
Base Size: 25x25mm, Crushing Strength (1), Yellow-Bellied, *Slave Orcs are not Vicious*

The Orcs' great strength and brutal ferocity are an asset to any army, and the Abyssal Dwarfs push vast hordes of enslaved brutes towards the enemy before committing their own troops.

Gargoyles * Infantry

Unit Size	Sp	Me	Ra	De	Att	Ne	Pts
Troop (10)	10	4+	–	3+	8	9/11	80

Special
Base Size: 25x25mm, Fly, Regeneration (3+)

These dumb creatures always follow the armies of the Abyssal Dwarfs, hanging in the sky like a sinister pall, ready to plunge with voracious appetite onto wounded warriors and stragglers.

Slave Orc Gore Riders * Cavalry

Unit Size	Sp	Me	Ra	De	At	Ne	Pts
Troop (5)	8	4+	–	4+	8	9/11	85
Regiment (10)	8	4+	–	4+	16	12/14	130

Special
Crushing Strength (1), Thunderous Charge (1), Yellow-Bellied, Slave Orcs are not Vicious

Being tough, capable and eager to fight, Orcs make ideal slave soldiers, and none more so than the Gore Riders. Saddled atop their bestial mounts and capable of covering ground at a punishing rate, these primitive cavalry hit the opposition like a solid brick wall, pulverising lesser troops entirely and bringing even elites to their knees.

Lesser Obsidian Golems Large Infantry

Unit Size	Sp	Me	Ra	De	Att	Ne	Pts
Regiment (3)	5	4+	–	6+	9	–/14	135
Horde (6)	5	4+	–	6+	18	–/17	210

Special
Base Size: 50x50mm, Height 3, Crushing Strength (2), Shambling

Soulless constructs animated by the dark powers of the Iron-casters, these automatons are slow and dim-witted, but extremely strong and almost indestructible.

Abyssal Halfbreeds Cavalry

Unit Size	Sp	Me	Ra	De	Att	Ne	Pts
Troop (5)	8	3+	–	4+	8	11/13	125
Regiment (10)	8	3+	–	4+	16	14/16	195

Special
Crushing Strength (1), Regeneration (5+), Thunderous Charge (1)

These debased monstrosities, product of the Iron-casters' insane crossbreeding experiments, often have the body of a quadrupedal Abyssal creature and the upper torso of a Dwarf.

Greater Obsidian Golem Monster

Unit Size	Sp	Me	Ra	De	Att	Ne	Pts
1	5	4+	–	6+	8	–/18	160

Special
Crushing Strength (3), Shambling

Black stone-giants that tower over the battlefield, these monsters thunder against the enemy under the control of the Iron-casters that animated them.

Abyssal Grotesques Large Cavalry

Unit Size	Sp	Me	Ra	De	Att	Ne	Pts
Regiment (3)	7	4+	–	5+	9	12/14	165
Horde (6)	7	4+	–	5+	18	16/18	250

Special
Brutal, Crushing Strength (2), Regeneration (5+), Thunderous Charge (1)

Huge Abyssal hybrids, the Grotesques are tougher and more powerful than the other Halfbreeds.

G'rog Mortar — War Engine

Unit Size	Sp	Me	Ra	De	Att	Ne	Pts
1	4	–	5+	5+	1	10/12	100

Special

Blast (D6+2), Indirect Fire, Piercing (2), Reload!

The most common guns in the service of the Abyssal Dwarfs, these versatile weapons are used both in sieges and on the battlefield, where they make it almost suicidal for the enemies to concentrate their forces.

'Dragon' Fire-team — War Engine

Unit Size	Sp	Me	Ra	De	Att	Ne	Pts
1	4	–	–	4+	10	10/12	50

Special

Base Size: 25x50mm, Breath Attack (Att), Individual

This fiendish weapon consists of a team of two, carrying a canister of a highly volatile, flammable liquid with a pipe coming from it, which is used to project great gouts of alchemical fire into the ranks of the enemy.

Katsuchan Rocket Launcher — War Engine

Unit Size	Sp	Me	Ra	De	Att	Ne	Pts
1	4	–	5+	5+	3	10/12	85

Special

Blast (D3), Indirect Fire, Piercing (1), Reload!

At the start of an engagement, the Katsuchans unleash a relentless bombardment that is used to force the hand of the enemy, leaving them no choice but to retreat or advance into the waiting Decimators and Blacksouls.

Angkor Heavy Mortar — War Engine

Unit Size	Sp	Me	Ra	De	Att	Ne	Pts
1	4	–	5+	5+	1	10/12	120

Special

Blast (D6+4), Indirect Fire, Piercing (3), Reload!

The Angkor mortar is a large artillery piece that fires huge shells filled with the explosive concoctions of the Iron-casters – any regiment it hits directly disappears in a cloud of smoke.

Overmaster   Hero (Inf)

Unit Size	Sp	Me	Ra	De	Att	Ne	Pts
1	4	3+	–	6+	5	13/15	120

Special

Crushing Strength (1), Individual, Inspiring

The generals of the Abyssal Dwarf armies are ruthless, cunning and armed with mighty tools of destruction and thick magical armour of obsidian and cast iron.

Overmaster on Great Abyssal Dragon   Hero (Mon)

Unit Size	Sp	Me	Ra	De	Att	Ne	Pts
1	10	3+	–	5+	8	17/19	280

Special

Breath Attack (10), Crushing Strength (3) Fly, Inspiring

Huge, winged, Abyss-spawned nightmares are often used as steeds by the highest-ranking Iron-casters and Overmasters.

Slavedriver   Hero (Inf)

Unit Size	Sp	Me	Ra	De	Att	Ne	Pts
1	4	5+	–	5+	1	10/12	50

Special

Individual, Inspiring

The cruel symbols born on the banners of the Abyssal Dwarfs are often the last thing many folk see as free individuals.

Abyssal Halfbreed Champion   Hero (Cav)

Unit Size	Sp	Me	Ra	De	Att	Ne	Pts
1	8	3+	–	5+	6	12/14	160

Special

Crushing Strength (3), Individual, Inspiring, Regeneration (5+)

The greatest amongst the Halfbreeds are given great two-handed hammers and axes, and let loose against the enemy before their fury takes over and they endanger their own side.

Abyssal Grotesque Champion — Hero (Lrg Cav)

Unit Size	Sp	Me	Ra	De	Att	Ne	Pts
1	7	3+	–	5+	5	12/14	140

Special

Brutal, Crushing Strength (2), Nimble, Regeneration (5+), Thunderous Charge (1)

The largest and most powerful of the Grotesques make for formidable killing machines.

Iron-caster — Hero (Inf)

Unit Size	Sp	Me	Ra	De	Att	Ne	Pts
1	4	4+	–	5+	2	11/13	105

Special

Crushing Strength (1), Fireball (6), Heal (3 – works only on War Engines, Golems and Immortal Guard), Individual, Inspiring (War Engines only)

Options

• Lightning Bolt (3) for +20 pts

• Surge (8) for +15 pts

The Iron-casters wield the twisted fire-magic of Ariagful, evil Queen of the Black Flame.

Supreme Iron-caster on Great Winged Halfbreed — Hero (Mon)

Unit Size	Sp	Me	Ra	De	Att	Ne	Pts
1	10	4+	–	5+	5	15/17	190

Special

Crushing Strength (2), Fireball (10), Fly, Heal (4 – works only on War Engines, Golems and Immortal Guard), Inspiring

Options

• Lightning Bolt (3) for +20 pts

• Surge (10) for +20 pts

This evil spellcaster can channel the hellish energies of the Abyss and shape them into horrible sorceries and summoning rituals.

Ba'su'su the Vile [1] — Hero (Inf)

Unit Size	Sp	Me	Ra	De	Att	Ne	Pts
1	10	3+	–	5+	8	15/17	220

Special

Base Size: 25x25mm, Crushing Strength (2), Fly, Individual, Inspiring (Gargoyles only), Regeneration (5+)

Vile Spawn

If your army includes Ba'su'su, for +20 pts you may upgrade a single unit of Gargoyles to represent his flock of elder Gargoyles. This unit has Defence 4+ and Crushing Strength (1).

A halfbreed of great power, Ba'su'su the Vile, is a mighty pinioned monster, tormented by the low status his halfbreed nature condemns him to.

Brakki Barka [1] — Hero (Cav)

Unit Size	Sp	Me	Ra	De	At	Ne	Pts
1	8	3+	–	5+	6	14/16	200

Special

Bhardoom!, Crushing Strength (3), Individual, Regeneration (5+)

Bhardoom!

Because of his awesome battle-cry, and what that means to his own troops, Brakki Barka is Extremely Inspiring (this is the same as the Inspiring special rule, except that it has a range of 12").

Barka leads from the front and while he is nominally the Lord of the Legion of Bardoom, his battle orders are a single bellow of the word 'Bhardoom', that roars impossibly loud over the entire field of battle.

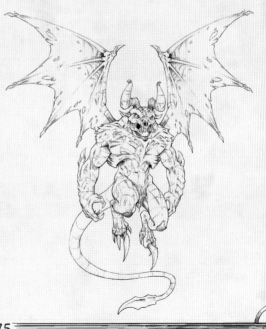

GOBLIN ARMIES

No scholar has yet offered a convincing account of the moment or method by which Goblins came into being. The fabric of their history is so closely woven into that of Orcs as to be all but indistinguishable, and few early records exist where one is mentioned without the other. It is a common mockery to suggest that Garkan the Black created Goblins with 'whatever was left' after Orcs were made – and perhaps, given their renowned propensity for scavenging and invention, this slur would not displease them. While they may at times be seen merely as the oil that lubricates the wheels of the Orc army, what they lack in stature or strength they more than make up for in sheer number, ingenuity and savage cruelty. Whether under the lash of their Orc masters, or banded together in their own harrowing war-parties, it is a fool who underestimates the Goblin.

Goblin Army Special Rules

Alignment: Evil

Utterly Spineless
All units in this list have the Yellow Bellied special rule, unless specified otherwise.

Goblins were once believed to have been Orc children – a laughable but forgivable assumption given their small frame, green skin, and the fact that to this day they are often to be found living among Orc tribes, albeit bitterly subservient and fearful of their larger, more capable cousins. As a group, an instinctive and almost rodent-like desire to propagate drives the Goblin to a constant, frenetic level of activity, fills him with a boundless energy for progressing the swarm ever onwards. Orcs shrewdly harness this dynamism to their own ends, but regularly perform culls to keep the population under control and avoid any potential uprising.

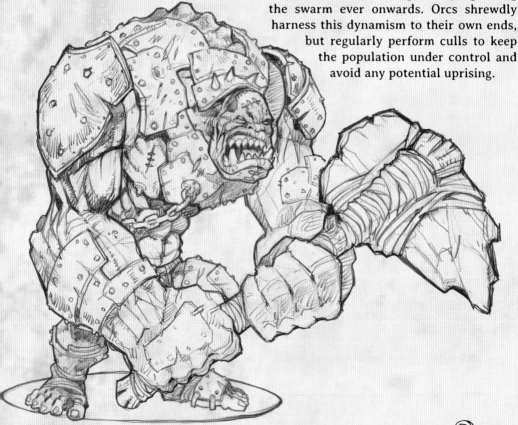

Left to their own devices, Goblins are prone to short tempers, mindless brutality and a characteristic array of other unpleasant neurological disharmonies. Try though they might, true sophistication always eludes them, and this is never more evident than when conversing with the more civilised races.

All too close to the surface lurks a barely suppressed twitch, a hair-triggered switch ready to be thrown, such that in the presence of a Goblin you always feel a misplaced word might land you on the leading edge of a jagged blade. They outstrip even Orcs in their capacity for perverse malice - seeking to persecute anything and anyone over which they can gain the upper hand, presumably an outlet for the pent up frustration of finding themselves so often last in the pecking order.

Unlike the predominantly destructive Orcs, the Goblin race is a great maker of things. Perhaps fuelled largely by their own physical inadequacies or hierarchical shortcomings, they apply their quick and energetic minds to the conception of occasionally baffling contraptions – usually designed to cause harm in

unthinkable ways, or to otherwise levy some sinister confrontational advantage. However, they often lack the practiced eye, the proper concentration or the true craftsmanship to fully convert these ideas into reality without severe ineloquence or misjudged consequences.

That said, so prolific are the attempts that several of the instruments of war found in both Orc and Ogre armies are in fact Goblin-made. Goblins also differ from their larger, more brutish cousins in terms of individual courage, for Goblins possess none of it. Where Orcs will stand and fight to the bitter end of a gruesome battle, the Goblin contingent will have long since fled in cowardice (often avoiding the axes of both the enemy and their Orc masters alike) the moment the tide seemed to be turning against them.

But not all Goblins live by the tyranny of the Orcs, with some deserting to form scattered, petty kingdoms, appointing leaders and living by their own rule. Varying in size, these crude shanty villages are set up rapidly on the outskirts of whatever civilised settlement the Goblins in question wish to scavenge from, harassing supply caravans until they are driven off by local militia and forced to relocate. However, this does not tell the whole story, for the location of far too few such villages is known at any given time to possibly account for so apparently numerous a race as the Goblins.

The truth is that Goblins are proficient at tunnelling, and usually do so not long after setting up camp, able to dwell below ground for long periods and thus inadvertently concealing their true number. While below, they will be sustained by whatever poor creatures they manage to drag down with them, carcasses scraped clean of flesh and gristle alike, bones sucked dry of marrow. No Dwarf will admit it, and it is still the cause of short fuses whenever the two races meet, but impressively vast, albeit primitive warrens of narrow passageways, nauseating crawl-spaces and (only slightly) larger dwelling-bores lurk below ground in many parts of Mantica.

In this way, unlike the rigorously census-monitored human population of Mantica, no-one really knows exactly how many Goblins inhabit the realm, but popular perception suggests that they are worryingly underestimated. However, just as with the incessant rats that plague the under-streets of the great Basilean cities, making frequent, unwelcome incursions into civilised life, this is a thought that most would sooner dismiss than dwell on. For some fear that if left unopposed the Goblins might one day reach some kind of critical mass, swarming across the realm in a flood to rival even that at the end of The Age of Ice. Such concerned citizens increasingly call upon their leaders to suppress what has become known as 'the Goblin threat'.

A Goblin plan is hastily formed, and tends toward immediate, exacting effect rather than lasting strategy. When shepherded into war, Goblins take to the rapture of battle and with a sickening relish, so long as they believe they hold an advantage over the enemy. Their preferred tactics involve the use of superior numbers, ranged or surprise attacks, or better still letting allies such as Giants and Trolls do the fighting.

Recognising this and having learned that even the slaughtering of deserters is no guarantee of overcoming their pathological cowardice, both Orc and Goblin leaders

tend to organise their kin into large, sprawling rabbles – each an overbearingly noisy blur of brandished blades. The sensation of being among a large number of their own kind gives the Goblins a heady delusion of grandeur, and in this state they can be whipped up into an alarmingly effective wave, ready to crash against the front line of an advancing enemy or engulf and overpower a single, unfortunate target.

In smaller groups, a similar illusion of invulnerability can be conjured by equipping the Goblin with shields and sharpsticks, or with ranged weapons, war-machines, and in some cases hulking bestial mounts of terrifying ferocity. All of these augmentations the Goblin will embrace keenly, and thusly equipped will carry out his bloody duty with unnerving glee. That is, for as long as his resolve remains unshaken, which, much to the dismay of his commanders, is not usually very long.

Sharpsticks
Infantry

Unit Size	Sp	Me	Ra	De	Att	Ne	Pts
Regiment (20)	5	5+	–	4+	15	12/14	95
Horde (40)	5	5+	–	4+	30	19/21	155
Legion (60)	5	5+	–	4+	35	25/27	230

Special

Phalanx

The best Goblin warriors (i.e. those that stand their ground at least once against the enemy) are armed with long spiky sticks, which better suit their mainly defensive combat style.

Spitters
Infantry

Unit Size	Sp	Me	Ra	De	Att	Ne	Pts
Regiment (20)	5	6+	5+	3+	10	12/14	85
Horde (40)	5	6+	5+	3+	20	19/21	140

Special

Bows

Goblins have a natural preference for keeping their distance and peppering the enemy with missile weapons, so these diminutive archers are the most valued troops of Goblindom.

Rabble
Infantry

Unit Size	Sp	Me	Ra	De	Att	Ne	Pts
Regiment (20)	5	5+	–	4+	12	12/14	75
Horde (40)	5	5+	–	4+	25	19/21	125
Legion (60)	5	5+	–	4+	30	25/27	180

Equipped with scraps of armour and shields of all shapes and sizes picked up from the debris of battle, and armed with a mix of rusty, blunted blades, the Goblin Rabble are not exactly elite troops.

Mawbeasts Pack *
Cavalry

Unit Size	Sp	Me	Ra	De	Att	Ne	Pts
Troop (5)	6	3+	–	3+	6	9/11	60
Regiment (10)	6	3+	–	3+	12	12/14	95

Special

Height 1, Crushing Strength (1), Nimble, Vicious

Note that handlers models are purely decorative.

The Mawbeasts are ferocious critters goaded into battle by their Goblin handlers.

Fleabag Riders — Cavalry

Unit Size	Sp	Me	Ra	De	Att	Ne	Pts
Troop (5)	10	4+	–	4+	7	9/11	95
Regiment (10)	10	4+	–	4+	14	12/14	145
Horde (20)	10	4+	–	4+	28	17/19	255

Special
Thunderous Charge (1), Nimble

Goblins give the name 'Fleabags' to any beast they manage to tame enough to ride: giant rodents, ferocious wolves or even horrid giant bugs.

Fleabag Chariots — Large Cavalry

Unit Size	Sp	Me	Ra	De	Att	Ne	Pts
Regiment (3)	9	4+	5+	4+	8	10/12	110
Horde (6)	9	4+	5+	4+	16	13/15	170

Special
Bows, Base Size: 50x100mm, Thunderous Charge (2)

Goblin Chariots have bows, but rather unusually for Goblins, they also seem to like driving at high speed into enemy regiments.

Fleabag Rider Sniffs — Cavalry

Unit Size	Sp	Me	Ra	De	Att	Ne	Pts
Troop (5)	10	5+	5+	3+	7	9/11	95
Regiment (10)	10	5+	5+	3+	14	12/14	145

Special
Bows, Nimble

These mounted Goblin archers excel at lightning hit and run attacks.

Trolls — Large Infantry

Unit Size	Sp	Me	Ra	De	Att	Ne	Pts
Regiment (3)	6	4+	–	5+	9	11/14	125
Horde (6)	6	4+	–	5+	18	14/17	190

Special
Crushing Strength (2), Regeneration (5+)

Note that Trolls are not Yellow Bellied, as that would require too much intelligence on their part.

Trolls are large, feral humanoids whose appearance varies considerably depending on the environment they live in. However, all Trolls have dim wits and an insatiable appetite.

Sharpstick Thrower — War Engine

Unit Size	Sp	Me	Ra	De	Att	Ne	Pts
1	5	–	5+	4+	2	8/10	55

Special

Blast (D3), Piercing (2), Reload!

This crude bolt thrower allows its crew to 'stick' the enemy from a reasonably safe distance – this explains the huge number of volunteers that vie for this role in battle.

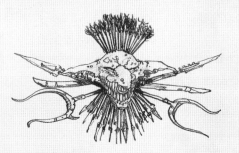

War-Trombone — War Engine

Unit Size	Sp	Me	Ra	De	Att	Ne	Pts
1	5	–	–	4+	12	8/10	65

Special

Breath Attack (Att), Piercing (1)

Certainly less reassuring than a sharpstick thrower because of its considerably more limited range, the war-trombones are still quite popular because these huge wheeled blunderbusses can unleash terrible destruction amongst the enemy.

Big Rocks Thrower — War Engine

Unit Size	Sp	Me	Ra	De	Att	Ne	Pts
1	5	–	5+	4+	1	8/10	80

Special

Blast (D6+2), Indirect Fire, Piercing (3), Reload!

Crewing one of these catapults is the ultimate fun for a Goblin, as the great cheers that accompany each shot can attest.

Mincer — Monster

Unit Size	Sp	Me	Ra	De	Att	Ne	Pts
1	5	4+	–	4+	(D6+6)*	9/11	80

Special

Base Size: 50x100mm, Height 3, Big Shield, Brutal, Thunderous Charge (3),

* Roll for the number of Attacks every time you resolve a melee.

The Mincer is essentially a carriage powered by the frantic labour of Goblins or a small steam engine. The rear sports a large counterweight, necessary to offset the huge weight of the Mincer itself, a large, cone of counter-rotating segments.

An adaptation of a digging machine, the Mincer's grinding cone is fitted with blades, its purpose to be sent hurtling at high speed down a tunnel packed with Dwarfs. The Mincer's cone is thick enough to deflect a cannon shot, so it usually manages to hit the Dwarf lines and live up to its name…

Giant
Monster

Unit Size	Sp	Me	Ra	De	Att	Ne	Pts
1	7	4+	–	5+	(D6+6)*	17/19	190

Special

Brutal, Crushing Strength (3), Fury, Strider.

Note that Giants are not Yellow Bellied, as that would require too much intelligence on their part.

* Roll for the number of Attacks every time you resolve a melee.

The brain of a Giant is way too small to properly control the creature's huge body. However, when goaded in the right direction, these dumb brutes are a terrible threat to any foe.

Slasher
Monster

Unit Size	Sp	Me	Ra	De	Att	Ne	Pts
1	7	4+	–	5+	8	14/16	165

Special

Crushing Strength (2), Thunderous Charge (1)

Note that Slashers are not Yellow Bellied.

Options

• Mount a small sharpstick thrower on it – Range 36", Ra 5+, 2 ranged attacks, Piercing (2) – for +10 pts.

A small crew of particularly brave (insane?) Goblins riding atop a wooden platform unsteadily strapped onto the back of a giant Slasher... with a sharpstick thrower on it!

King
Hero (Inf)

Unit Size	Sp	Me	Ra	De	Att	Ne	Pts
1	5	4+	4+	4+	5	11/13	90

Special

Bow, Individual, Inspiring

Options

• Mount on a Fleabag, increasing Speed to 10 (+20 pts) and changing to Hero (Cav)

Every so often, a Biggit will arise with grander ambitions than bossing around the members of his tribe. These individuals, touched by either the gods or madness (or possibly both) will have a vision, of the Goblin race overrunning all others and ruling supreme. These individuals will declare themselves the Goblin King, and will demand fealty from all other Goblins as the rightful supreme leader of their kind. The fact that there are many millions of Goblins in the world, and that at any one time, at least half a dozen such Biggits will exist, generating even more infighting between tribes, is possibly one of the reasons that Goblins are simultaneously so dangerous and so utterly unable to fulfil their potential.

King on Chariot
Hero (Lrg Cav)

Unit Size	Sp	Me	Ra	De	Att	Ne	Pts
1	9	4+	4+	5+	7	13/15	130

Special

Bow, Base Size: 50x100mm, Inspiring, Thunderous Charge (2)

This King likes to ride in style, it's also quite good for fleeing at speed...

Flaggit
Hero (Inf)

Unit Size	Sp	Me	Ra	De	Att	Ne	Pts
1	5	6+	–	4+	1	8/10	40

Special

Individual, Inspiring

Options

• Mount on a Fleabag, increasing Speed to 10 (+15 pts) and changing to Hero (Cav)

The job of carrying one of the sorcerous Wizbanners is very sought-after, as it involves staying well away from the enemy.

Biggit
Hero (Inf)

Unit Size	Sp	Me	Ra	De	Att	Ne	Pts
1	5	4+	4+	4+	3	9/11	60

Special

Bow, Individual, Inspiring

Options

• Mount on a Fleabag, increasing Speed to 10 (+15 pts) and changing to Hero (Cav)

The largest Goblins boss around their smaller brethren in a fashion reminiscent of the Orcs they want to emulate.

Wiz
Hero (Inf)

Unit Size	Sp	Me	Ra	De	Att	Ne	Pts
1	5	5+	–	4+	1	9/11	45

Special

Individual, Lightning Bolt (3)

Options

• Wind Blast (5) for +15pts
• Bane-chant (2) for +15pts
• Fireball (6) for +15pts
• Mount on a Fleabag, increasing Speed to 10 (+15 pts) and changing to Hero (Cav)

The spellcasters of Goblinkind are known as the Wiz, all of whom are diminutive but dangerous.

Troll Bruiser
Hero (Lrg Inf)

Unit Size	Sp	Me	Ra	De	Att	Ne	Pts
1	6	3+	–	5+	5	12/15	125

Special

Crushing Strength (3), Inspiring (Trolls only), Nimble, Regeneration (5+)

Note that Trolls are not *Yellow Bellied*.

Bigger and nastier than the others...

Magwa & Jo'os [1]
Hero (Lrg Cav)

Unit Size	Sp	Me	Ra	De	Att	Ne	Pts
1	6	3+	–	4+	4	12/14	110

Special

Both models should be mounted together on a 50x50mm base, Height 1, Crushing Strength (2), Individual, Inspiring, Lightning Bolt (4), Vicious

Note that the Yellow Bellied rule in this case represents Magwa's troubles controlling his ferocious pet!

The Magwa'ns

If your army includes Magwa and Jo'os, a single Mawbeast Pack in the army is no longer Irregular – they are the Magwa'ns, a group of enthusiastic, would-be successors to the role of Jo'os handler if (when) Jo'os is finally going to devour Magwa.

Magwa was a simple Mawbeast handler until the day he found a magical sharpstick in an abandoned Troll's lair. The powerful artefact allowed him to subdue and gain control of the mightiest of Mawbeasts – the terrible Jo'os.

ORC ARMIES

It is often remarked out of hand that Orcs appear to have been bred for war. What few realise is that this is quite literally true. This race of thuggish, brutal creatures who revel in violence and murder was the product of the Wicked one known as Arkhan the Black, the dark aspect of the essence of Smithying. As the God War raged, with little to choose between either side, the various Wicked Ones plotted and schemed to try and tip the balance in favour of out-and-out anarchy. Some sought to manipulate the hearts of men, others to sow the seeds of disruption amongst the Elder races. Arkhan embarked on a more direct route, seeking to create a new race which would make war on all others.

Taking the bodies and souls of various sentient creatures, Arkhan deconstructed them all and began his work, hammering away at his dark soul forges and horrific flesh anvils, twisting these natural building blocks into a whole new terrifying aspect. What emerged after 900 days, blinking and agonised in the light of the real world, was a race with only one goal ever in its collective consciousness – the destruction of all it came across.

Orc Army Special Rules

Alignment: Evil

Tribal Might
All units in this list have Crushing Strength (1), unless specified otherwise.

Also, all infantry models in this list are on 25x25mm bases, unless specified otherwise.

Goblin Stabby Sneak
Goblin Stabby Sneaks are tiny treacherous assassins of uncommon bravado.

This unit has +1 attack.

Goblin Zappy Sneak
Zappy Sneaks are clever little imps gifted with nasty and unpredictable magical powers.

This unit has the Lightning Bolt (2) spell.

Orcs are often said to take pleasure only in destruction and death, but this is not entirely true. Driven as they are by internal agonies of a physical and spiritual nature, it would be truer to say that good, purity and order are actually painful to them in a very real sense, and they lash out at them as a reflex. Orcs do not know themselves why this is – self-awareness not being a particular requirement of their creator – all they know is the bone-deep need to crush everything which they see before them, to reach out and destroy and in so doing to find momentary catharsis from the agony which otherwise consumes them.

Though the God War ended centuries ago, the Orcs endured. Their unnatural resilience and propensity for violence ensured that they carved out fluid though sizeable domains on the edges of civilisation, colonising those places where

no other race cared or was able to settle. Their natural drives mean that peace is an alien concept, and if confronted with no other foe, they will often fall to fighting amongst themselves. Few among their number are able to focus on anything more than the next fight, and this leads to one of the more curious paradoxes of the Orc race. Their leaders, those who exhibit enough cunning and forethought to be able to plan and conceive of ideas beyond pure, blind aggression, are often great and powerful thinkers in their crude way. It takes iron will and sharp wits as well as sheer brute force to control even a small number of Orcs, and the Warlords of some of the larger tribes in the world would rival some of the greatest generals of Men, Dwarfs and Elves in their capacity for strategy.

Such individuals are thankfully rare, and once killed, their carefully welded alliances of Orcs will fall quickly into disarray and indiscipline. It is this fact alone which keeps Orcs from sweeping all civilisations

before them and ruling supreme. It is unclear whether Arkhan, in those dark and desperate days at his forges, intended this as a function of maintaining the imbalance of the God War and the world that would emerge from it, or whether pure chance gave the world this respite. Whichever is the case, what is clear is that the Orcs, whatever their original purpose, are very much here to stay.

The Orc

Physically, Orcs are tremendously imposing. Their bodies are comparable in basic silhouette and size to a large man, though the details vastly differ. Huge, underslung jaws contain rows of sharp teeth. A protruding brow surmounts deep set, bloodshot eyes. The nose is more a snout, and Orcs have very little sense of smell, explaining perhaps the appalling stench of their encampments. Their bodies are hugely muscled and powerful, covered in tough green hide, akin to the leather armour of some steppes warriors.

Their capacity for pain and privation is unmatched by any other race in the world. They can march for weeks on little to no sustenance, fight for days with no sign of tiring and survive wounds that should rightly kill them. Every aspect of their repulsive physicality is crafted to keep them alive and fighting as long as possible, from their unnaturally resilient flesh to their thick, green-black blood which flows slowly through their veins and means even the most grave of wounds will not slow them.

Orcs do not have a 'society' as such, operating in roaming bands from a few dozen to several thousand strong. Their inability to settle in one place derives from their very nature. Orcs must always be active and engaged, and it is this which drives them to fight amongst themselves when no other foe presents itself. Thus, it is the largest and most cunning Orcs who naturally rise to the top, and the greatest warlords of the race are terrifying brutes, their size matched only by their ferocity and cunning. Such individuals, when they arise, will grow to lead great hordes of their kin, raiding and pillaging any settlement or civilisation they come across until such time as the Warlord is inevitably killed. When this happens, the discipline within the Orc ranks will quickly crumble, leaving a disorganised and splintered mass of Orcs to squabble among themselves.

This fluidity could only work for Orcs, fitting with their own natural and reflexive distaste for order and peace. There are no fixed 'tribes' or 'clans' amongst the Orc race, and an Orc warrior will often fight under many banners over the course of a long and violent life. This is both the blessing and the curse bestowed upon the world by Arkhan – a race that will never conquer all others, but will forever remain as an open wound, dragging at them, and ensuring that no one race reigns supreme.

Ax — Infantry

Unit Size	Sp	Me	Ra	De	Att	Ne	Pts
Troop (10)	5	4+	–	5+	10	9/11	90
Regiment (20)	5	4+	–	5+	12	13/15	125
Horde (40)	5	4+	–	5+	25	20/22	205

Named after the vicious axes they carry, the orcs forming the core regiments of the Orc hordes also carry sharpened, spiked shields that are as much a weapon as protection.

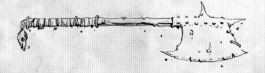

Morax — Infantry

Unit Size	Sp	Me	Ra	De	Att	Ne	Pts
Troop (10)	5	3+	–	4+	20	10/12	140
Regiment (20)	5	3+	–	4+	25	14/16	200

Experts in fighting with a large axe in each hand with uncanny ease, these ruthless veterans are a fearsome foe.

Greatax — Infantry

Unit Size	Sp	Me	Ra	De	Att	Ne	Pts
Troop (10)	5	3+	–	4+	10	10/12	100
Regiment (20)	5	3+	–	4+	12	14/16	145
Horde (40)	5	3+	–	4+	25	21/23	240

Special
Crushing Strength (2)

The toughest, strongest Orcs discard their shields, so that they can have both hands free to wield the huge two-handed cleavers they call 'greatax'.

Gore Riders — Cavalry

Unit Size	Sp	Me	Ra	De	Att	Ne	Pts
Troop (5)	8	3+	–	5+	8	10/12	120
Regiment (10)	8	3+	–	5+	16	13/15	185

Special
Thunderous Charge (1)

Gores need little reason to disembowel anyone that gets too close, making them perfect battle-mounts for bloodthirsty Orcs.

Gore Chariots — Large Cavalry

Unit Size	Sp	Me	Ra	De	Att	Ne	Pts
Regiment (3)	7	3+	–	5+	9	11/13	140
Horde (6)	7	3+	–	5+	18	14/16	215

Special
Base Size: 50x100mm, Thunderous Charge (2)

Sometimes a pair of Gores is attached to a war-chariot carrying a couple of Orcs armed to the teeth. Their tactic is simple: charge at the nearest enemy regiment.

Skulks — Infantry

Unit Size	Sp	Me	Ra	De	Att	Ne	Pts
Troop (10)	6	5+	5+	3+	8	9/11	75

Special
Bows, Vanguard

Skulk is the name the Orcs give to those amongst their number who – for some unfathomable reason – like to use bows. Orcs tend to view these individuals as strange, even cowardly, though many Orc warlords can see the usefulness of having archers who are less likely to run away or simply be squished like Goblins.

Orclings* — Large Infantry

Unit Size	Sp	Me	Ra	De	Att	Ne	Pts
Regiment (3)	5	5+	–	3+	12	10/12	60
Horde (6)	5	5+	–	3+	24	13/15	90

Special
Height 0, Vicious,
Orclings do not have Crushing Strength

Malevolent imps of very little consequence, but source of very great irritation for everyone.

Trolls* — Large Infantry

Unit Size	Sp	Me	Ra	De	Att	Ne	Pts
Regiment (3)	6	4+	–	5+	9	11/14	125
Horde (6)	6	4+	–	5+	18	14/17	190

Special
Crushing Strength (2), Regeneration (5+)

Trolls are large, feral humanoids whose appearance varies considerably depending on the environment they live in. However, all Trolls have dim wits and an insatiable appetite.

Fight Wagons — Large Cavalry

Unit Size	Sp	Me	Ra	De	Att	Ne	Pts
Regiment (3)	7	3+	–	5+	15	11/13	170
Horde (6)	7	3+	–	5+	30	14/16	260

Special
Base Size: 50x100mm

These bizarre contraptions consist of a wheeled platform crammed full with eager Morax at the front, pushed by two gores enclosed in an armoured compartment at the back.

War Drum — Monster

Unit Size	Sp	Me	Ra	De	Att	Ne	Pts
1	5	4+	–	4+	3	-/11	80

Special
Height 1, Great Thunder

Great Thunder
While within 6" of one or more war drums, friendly non-allied units have +2 to their waver and rout nerve values. War Drums themselves are not affected by this rule.

The booming of Orc war drums in the distance is a terrible omen of the destruction to come.

Giant — Monster

Unit Size	Sp	Me	Ra	De	Att	Ne	Pts
1	7	4+	–	5+	D6+6*	17/19	190

Special
Brutal, Crushing Strength (3), Fury, Strider

* Roll for the number of Attacks every time you resolve a melee.

A Giant is a huge humanoid, a veritable mountain of bone, sinew and flesh with a very, very tiny brain and a massive appetite.

Krudger — Hero (Inf)

Unit Size	Sp	Me	Ra	De	Att	Ne	Pts
1	5	3+	–	5+	5	12/14	130

Special
Crushing Strength (2), Individual, Inspiring

Options
- Mount on a Gore, increasing Speed to 8 (+20 pts) and changing to Hero (Cav)
- Goblin Stabby Sneak (+15 pts)
- Goblin Zappy Sneak (+15 pts)

The Krudgers have managed to make it to the top of Orc society.

Krudger on Gore Chariot — Hero (Lrg Cav)

Unit Size	Sp	Me	Ra	De	Att	Ne	Pts
1	7	3+	–	5+	7	14/16	185

Special
Base Size: 50x100mm, Crushing Strength (2), Inspiring, Thunderous Charge (2)

Options
- Goblin Stabby Sneak (+15 pts)
- Goblin Zappy Sneak (+15 pts)

Gore chariots make less impressive rides than a slasher for an Orc general, but are much safer...

Krudger on Slasher — Hero (Mon)

Unit Size	Sp	Me	Ra	De	Att	Ne	Pts
1	7	3+	–	5+	10	16/18	235

Special
Crushing Strength (3), Inspiring

Options
- Mount on a Winged Slasher instead, increasing Speed to 10 and gaining the Fly special rule (+50 pts)

Almost as prized as their winged brethren, Slashers are giant carnivorous reptiles, all fangs, claws and bad attitude. Only an equally lethal Orc leader can think of using one as a mount.

Flagger — Hero (Inf)

Unit Size	Sp	Me	Ra	De	Att	Ne	Pts
1	5	4+	–	4+	1	9/11	50

Special
Individual, Inspiring

Options
- Mount on a Gore, increasing Speed to 8 (+15 pts) and changing to Hero (Cav)

Trying to convince these hand-picked Orc champions not to use the large implement they carry to hit the enemy on the head is not difficult... it's pointless.

Godspeaker — Hero (Inf)

Unit Size	Sp	Me	Ra	De	Att	Ne	Pts
1	5	3+	–	4+	2	10/12	75

Special

Fireball (9), Individual,

For every friendly non-allied Horde within 6", increase the amount of dice rolled for all spells by 1.

Options

• Bane Chant (2) for +15pts
• Heal (2) for +10pts
• Mount on a Gore, increasing Speed to 8 (+15 pts) and changing to Hero (Cav)

A mysterious summoner of the powers of the Orc gods of war.

Troll Bruiser — Hero (Large Inf)

Unit Size	Sp	Me	Ra	De	Att	Ne	Pts
1	6	3+	–	5+	5	12/15	125

Special

Crushing Strength (3), Inspiring (Trolls only), Nimble, Regeneration (5+)

Bigger and nastier than the others...

Gakamak [1] — Hero (Inf)

Unit Size	Sp	Me	Ra	De	At	Ne	Pts
1	5	2+	–	5+	7	13/15	210

Special

Crushing Strength (3), Individual, Very Inspiring, Vicious

Options

• Mount on a Gore, increasing Speed to 8 (+30 pts)

In battle, Gakamak the Smasher lives up to the title by which he is known and feared across the whole of northern Mantica. He is utterly unafraid of engaging even the most threatening enemy and has felled every foe from noble Elven Drakon Knights to the winged Abyssal demon known only as the Lord of Midnight.

Wip the Half-cast [1] — Hero (Inf)

Unit Size	Sp	Me	Ra	De	Att	Ne	Pts
1	6	4+	–	4+	1	11/13	90

Special

Elite, Heal (3), Individual, Inspiring (Orclings only), Lightning Bolt (3)

Note: Wip does not have Crushing Strength

Wip's Playmates

If your army includes Wip, for +5 points you may upgrade a single unit of Orclings to represent Wip's affectionate playmates and adorers. This unit has the Headstrong special rule.

Strange things keep happening around Wip... things connected with his bizarre powers, his frail yet agile body... and his pointy ears.

UNDEAD ARMIES

Necromancy is the most abhorrent of sorcery, and those who practise it are hated and feared in equal measure. In all civilised places, its use is outlawed. Those caught studying these black arts are likely to find themselves dragged in ensorcelled iron to a painful execution, but established Necromancers are never short of acolytes. Necromancy offers immortality to those who master it, never mind that few actually do, and that the price of failure is to be condemned for eternity to the endless cold and night of the Utterdark.

For that handful that escape detection and that succeed in their quest, such devotion does have its rewards - the most powerful Necromancers are all but immortal. In violation of natural law, Necromancers are able to use their power to defy death itself, extending their own lives virtually indefinitely. Furthermore, they are able to create armies to do their bidding and seize power of a more mundane sort. Invoking powers learnt from ancient tomes, they are able to make corpses clamber back to their feet, and skeletons claw their way up from ancient battlefields. The greatest Necromancers are able to raise armies numbering the tens of thousands, armies that never tire, never need feeding, and never disobey.

Necromancy is a hateful art. The souls of those risen by its black magics are dragged screaming from whatever afterlife they might inhabit and forced back into their decayed mortal frames. Trapped in prisons of decayed flesh, they can only watch as their new master uses their very essence as a fuel to drive their old body on as a magical automaton, hacking down the innocent. Worse by far is the fate of those imprisoned – if the vessel is destroyed, there is a good chance that the summoned soul will not be able to find its way back to its rest. Such benighted spirits wander Mantica in agony until laid to rest by priest or paladin, or are cast out into the Utterdark for all time. It is for this reason that its practice causes such revulsion in right-thinking folk.

Undead Army Special Rules

Alignment: Evil

Evil Dead
All units in this list have Lifeleech (1) unless specified otherwise.

Undead Giant Rats (or are they Dogs?)
These creatures follow the shambling hordes into battle, their venomous bites helping to spread the curse of the living death.

The unit increases its Lifeleech (1) to Lifeleech (2).

Of course, there are those wicked creatures, tormented in infernal planes of existence, who welcome a return to the land of the living, even if it is as an unfeeling corpse. These spirits are the most dangerous of a Necromancer's servants, for they obey him willingly and are thus allowed some measure of self-determination.

Ophidia is a hotbed of necromancy. In this ancient kingdom all manner of vile magical practises are condoned and encouraged. In Ophidia necromancy, demonology and other unnatural arts are studied like any other school of magic, and there necromancers are given high status. Far from being reviled, the people of that strange land worship the Necromancer-priests of the great temples. They can call back the dead, and so the common man sees for himself some measure of immortality. Ophidia is unusual in that its armies consist of undead and live warriors marching side by side, and its monumental buildings are raised by the labours of the dead. The Ophidians are bemused by the reactions of others to their dead magic, pointing out with some justification that necromancy helps to keep their kingdom mighty.

The work of Ophidia's dark scholars has unleashed many unclean things, close to the realm of death yet not truly dead, to prowl the dark. Both vampires and Ghouls are reckoned to be the products of the sorcerers of Ophidia, who, in searching for elixirs to grant immortality, have instead made monsters. Ghouls are little more than mindless beasts, but Vampires are truly dangerous. In their creation, the sorcerers of the desert were partially successful. Vampires are indeed immortal, barring the destruction of their body they cannot die, and even something as final-seeming as burning or dismemberment is no bar to continued life for the strongest of their number.

Time and again some vampire lords have been slain and their ashes dispersed, only for their corrupt souls to grow a new body in some forgotten crypt. This longevity is bought at great price. Although preternaturally swift and strong, their bodies are prone to bizarre afflictions. Some can not cross running water, or burst into fire at the touch of the sun. Many of them carry the stink of the charnel house around with them wherever they go, some are made bestial, some cannot speak. They hunger eternally for blood, and are inclined to terrible cruelty as they search for it. Many of them possess at least a grain of conscience, and are tormented by every life they take. Others immerse themselves in savagery, only to come to horrified realisation as to what they are every so often where they are tormented first by shame and guilt, and then by horror as their red thirst reasserts itself. Because of this many vampires are mad, and all suffer torments of the soul. Vampirism is a curse, bestowed as a gift.

Despite its many and hideous drawbacks, vampirism exerts a lure equal to that of necromancy. Vampires can be beautiful,

terrible and glorious, above the concerns of humanity, and powerful magicians in their own right. For this reason they are actively courted as often as they are hunted.

Ultimately, no good can come of Necromancy. It is the burden of all thinking, living things to come to terms with their mortality, and the existence of necromancy is yet another sign of Mantica's lack of balance. Like all dark magic Necromancy can be traced to the Abyss. There, at the bottom of the fiery pit, Durunjak, dark god of death, laughs every time an unwilling spirit is forced from heaven to suffer in a necrotic shell.

Skeleton Warriors — Infantry

Unit Size	Sp	Me	Ra	De	Att	Ne	Pts
Troop (10)	5	5+	–	4+	10	–/12	65
Regiment (20)	5	5+	–	4+	12	–/16	90
Horde (40)	5	5+	–	4+	25	–/23	150

Special
Shambling

Options
• Undead Giant Rats (Dogs?) (+10 pts)

The Necromancers and Vampires can rely on the Skeletons' unquestionable esprit de corpse.

Skeleton Spearmen — Infantry

Unit Size	Sp	Me	Ra	De	Att	Ne	Pts
Troop (10)	5	5+	–	4+	10	–/12	75
Regiment (20)	5	5+	–	4+	15	–/16	105
Horde (40)	5	5+	–	4+	30	–/23	175

Special
Phalanx, Shambling

Options
• Undead Giant Rats (Dogs?) (+10 pts)

Skeleton warriors that still remember how to form a hedge of sharp speartips.

Skeleton Archers — Infantry

Unit Size	Sp	Me	Ra	De	Att	Ne	Pts
Troop (10)	5	6+	5+	3+	8	–/12	75
Regiment (20)	5	6+	5+	3+	10	–/16	100
Horde (40)	5	6+	5+	3+	20	–/23	165

Special
Bows, Shambling

Options
• Undead Giant Rats (Dogs?) (+10 pts)

If a creature was a good shot in life, it can be raised from the grave with a modicum of its former skill. It's not a coincidence that most skeleton archers were once Elves.

Ghouls — Infantry

Unit Size	Sp	Me	Ra	De	Att	Ne	Pts
Troop (10)	6	4+	–	3+	10	8/10	65
Regiment (20)	6	4+	–	3+	12	12/14	90
Horde (40)	6	4+	–	3+	25	19/21	150

The ghouls are not strictly walking dead, but rather deranged cannibals and eaters of the dead that slowly lose their minds to the horror of their lives, turning into savage creatures half-human, half-undead.

Soul Reaver Infantry — Infantry

Unit Size	Sp	Me	Ra	De	Att	Ne	Pts
Troop (10)	6	3+	–	5+	20	11/13	180
Regiment (20)	6	3+	–	5+	25	15/17	260

Special
Crushing Strength (2), Lifeleech (2)

Vampires are an arrogant breed, and it follows that those who join their ranks tend to be the mightiest and vainest of their kind. Thus it is that many knights have fallen to the Vampire's curse, and now wander in eternal unlife, always looking to prove their sneering superiority to lesser, mortal creatures.

Soul Reaver Cavalry — Cavalry

Unit Size	Sp	Me	Ra	De	Att	Ne	Pts
Troop (5)	8	3+	–	6+	10	12/14	195
Regiment (10)	8	3+	–	6+	20	15/17	300

Special
Crushing Strength (1), Lifeleech (2),
Thunderous Charge (2)

The Soul Reavers are composed of Vampire knights, the most formidable living dead warriors – few enemies are brave enough to stand their ground against one of their devastating charges.

Revenants — Infantry

Unit Size	Sp	Me	Ra	De	Att	Ne	Pts
Troop (10)	5	4+	–	5+	10	–/13	85
Regiment (20)	5	4+	–	5+	12	–/17	120
Horde (40)	5	4+	–	5+	25	–/24	200

Special
Shambling

Options
• Exchange shields for two-handed weapons for free (lower Defence to 4+, gain Crushing Strength (1))
• Undead Giant Rats (Dogs?) (+10 pts)

Revenants are the reanimated remains of elite fighters, belonging to Guard regiments and other troops that were better equipped and trained than the average. This results in tougher, more skilled and more resilient undead warriors.

Revenant Cavalry — Cavalry

Unit Size	Sp	Me	Ra	De	Att	Ne	Pts
Troop (5)	8	4+	–	5+	8	–/14	110
Regiment (10)	8	4+	–	5+	16	–/17	170

Special
Shambling, Thunderous Charge (2)

The knights that have fallen fighting the undead are often condemned to renege their vows in the most odious of ways, feasting on the souls of those they had sworn to defend in life.

Wraiths
Infantry

Unit Size	Sp	Me	Ra	De	Att	Ne	Pts
Troop (10)	10	4+	–	6+	10	–/12	140
Regiment (20)	10	4+	–	6+	12	–/16	200

Special
Crushing Strength (1), Fly, Shambling

The souls of the most powerful enemies of the Vampires and Necromancers are cursed to a ghostly quasi-existence, serving their masters in death.

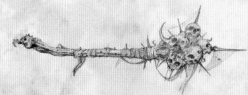

Mummies
Infantry

Unit Size	Sp	Me	Ra	De	Att	Ne	Pts
Troop (10)	5	4+	–	5+	10	–/14	120
Regiment (20)	5	4+	–	5+	12	–/18	170

Special
Crushing Strength (2), Regeneration (5+), Shambling.

The embalmed corpses of these ancient warriors from the southern deserts are slow, but almost impossible to destroy.

Zombies
Infantry

Unit Size	Sp	Me	Ra	De	Att	Ne	Pts
Regiment (20)	5	5+	–	3+	15	–/15	80
Horde (40)	5	5+	–	3+	30	–/22	130
Legion (60)	5	5+	–	3+	40	–/28	190

Special
Shambling

Options
• Undead Giant Rats (Dogs?) (+10 pts)

Zombies are freshly raised corpses, and their numbers grow exponentially during a campaign as the bodies of felled enemy soldiers and civilian victims alike swell their ranks.

Zombie Trolls
Large Infantry

Unit Size	Sp	Me	Ra	De	Att	Ne	Pts
Regiment (3)	6	4+	–	4+	9	-/15	115
Horde (6)	6	4+	–	4+	18	-/18	175

Special
Crushing Strength (2), Shambling.

Turning a Troll into a zombie improves their intelligence, but sadly at the expense of their ferocity and regenerating ability.

Werewolves — Large Infantry

Unit Size	Sp	Me	Ra	De	Att	Ne	Pts
Regiment (3)	9	3+	–	5+	9	12/14	160
Horde (6)	9	3+	–	5+	18	15/17	245

Special
Crushing Strength (1), Nimble

The curse of Lycanthropy turns its victims into huge wolf-hybrids, nigh-invulnerable to most weapons and fighting, with speed and strength beyond the limits of mortal flesh.

Wights — Large Infantry

Unit Size	Sp	Me	Ra	De	Att	Ne	Pts
Regiment (3)	6	4+	–	5+	9	-/14	155
Horde (6)	6	4+	–	5+	18	-/17	235

Special
Brutal, Crushing Strength (3), Shambling

Once mighty warrior kings of ancient times, Wights are creatures entirely of the supernatural. Where mortal creatures are constrained by the crude confines of physical flesh and blood, Wights are ethereal creatures who draw strength from their own spirit and legend. Freed from their earthly bindings, and soaked in the blood of the countless thousands of enemies they slayed in life, these creatures swell to massive proportions. Each stands the size of an Ogre, resplendent in ghostly armour and wielding two-handed spirit weapons. To face one is to face the myth of a warrior hero of the ages made manifest.

Balefire Catapult — War Engine

Unit Size	Sp	Me	Ra	De	Att	Ne	Pts
1	5	–	5+	4+	1	-/11	100

Special
Blast (D6+2), Indirect Fire, Piercing (2), *Reload!*, Shambling, Vicious

Certainly not precise or fast, the skeletons crewing these war machines are nevertheless more reliable than their living counterparts and totally relentless in their occupation.

Revenant King — Hero (Inf)

Unit Size	Sp	Me	Ra	De	Att	Ne	Pts
1	5	4+	–	5+	5	14/16	120

Special
Crushing Strength (1), Individual, Inspiring, Surge (6)

Options
• Mount on an undead horse, increasing Speed to 8 (+20 pts) and changing to Hero (Cav)

Buried in their barrows together with their most precious weapons and armour, the Revenant Kings make superb officers for the legions of Skeletons and Revenants.

Revenant King on Undead Wyrm — Hero (Mon)

Unit Size	Sp	Me	Ra	De	Att	Ne	Pts
1	7	4+	–	5+	9	18/20	190

Special
Crushing Strength (3), Surge (6), Inspiring

Options
• Mount on a Winged Wyrm, increasing Speed to 10 and gaining Fly (+45 pts).

A Great King of old buried together with its most mighty and faithful war-steed.

Undead Army Standard Bearer — Hero (Inf)

Unit Size	Sp	Me	Ra	De	Att	Ne	Pts
1	5	5+	–	4+	1	-/13	50

Special
Individual, Inspiring, Shambling

Options
• Mount on an undead horse, increasing Speed to 8 (+15 pts) and changing to Hero (Cav)

Most undead are uninterested in honour and duty, but the sorceries that imbue the gory standards of their armies are a source of unliving energy that sustains the minions of the Undead Lords.

Cursed Pharaoh

Hero (Inf)

Unit Size	Sp	Me	Ra	De	Att	Ne	Pts
1	5	3+	–	6+	5	15/17	145

Special

Crushing Strength (2), Individual, Inspiring, Regeneration (5+), Surge (6)

Driven by a willpower that conquered death itself centuries past, these fallen nobles are almost unstoppable in their unquenchable wrath. Great is their ire and the vengeance they exact on those that are greedy and foolish enough to dare violate their majestic burial complexes.

Vampire Lord

Hero (Inf)

Unit Size	Sp	Me	Ra	De	Att	Ne	Pts
1	7	3+	–	6+	8	14/16	220

Special

Crushing Strength (2), Individual, Inspiring, Lifeleech (2), Surge (3)

Options

• Heal (2) for +10pts

• Lightning Bolt (3) for +20pts

• Mount on an undead horse, increasing Speed to 9 (+15 pts) and changing to Hero (Cav)

These most powerful undead lords combine an unparalleled fighting ability with great necromantic powers.

Vampire on Undead Pegasus

Hero (Lrg Cav)

Unit Size	Sp	Me	Ra	De	Att	Ne	Pts
1	10	3+	–	5+	8	14/16	245

Special

Crushing Strength (2), Fly, Inspiring, Lifeleech (2), Surge (3)

Options

• Heal (2) for +10pts

• Lightning Bolt (3) for +20pts

An undead Pegasus allows the Vampire to move even faster across the battlefield.

Vampire on Undead Dragon

Hero (Mon)

Unit Size	Sp	Me	Ra	De	Att	Ne	Pts
1	10	3+	–	5+	10	17/19	330

Special

Breath Attack (10), Crushing Strength (3), Fly, Inspiring, Lifeleech (2), Surge (3)

Options

• Heal (2) for +10pts

• Lightning Bolt (3) for +20pts

The sight of one of these mighty creatures soaring above the battlefield is often enough to spread blind panic amongst the enemy.

Lykanis

Hero (Lrg Inf)

Unit Size	Sp	Me	Ra	De	Att	Ne	Pts
1	9	3+	–	5+	5	13/15	145

Special

Crushing Strength (2), Inspiring (Werewolves only), Nimble

The feral leader of the pack.

Lady Ilona [1]

Hero (Inf)

Unit Size	Sp	Me	Ra	De	At	Ne	Pts
1	8	3+	–	6+	8	14/16	280

Special

Crushing Strength (3), Heal (3), Individual, Inspiring, Lifeleech (2), Lightning Bolt (3), Surge (3)

The Promise of Love Eternal

Enemy Heroes attacking Lady Ilona receive –1 to hit in melee.

Even before she was gifted with the Vampire's curse, Ilona was renowned as a cruel, vain and capricious mistress in her own land and beyond. The day that she became a Vampire, all of those traits were magnified a thousandfold, and she slaughtered her own kin to take sole control of her realm. Ilona's contempt for anyone but herself extends even to her own dark kin, and her weapon of choice is a silvered greatsword, enchanted by countless dark blessings to be lethal to Vampires. Ilona seeks neither unity nor even dominion, but rather the extinction of every other living and unloving creature in the world. She is undoubtedly the most dangerous of her kind ever to walk the world.

Liche King

Hero (Inf)

Unit Size	Sp	Me	Ra	De	Att	Ne	Pts
1	5	5+	–	4+	1	14/16	145

Special

Individual, Inspiring, Regeneration (5+), Surge (12)

Options

- Heal (6) for +20pts, or free to replace Surge.
- Lightning Bolt (5) for +35pts
- Bane-chant (3) for +20pts
- Mount on an undead horse, increasing Speed to 8 (+20 pts) and changing to Hero (Cav)

Ancient kings who prolonged their wicked lives using forbidden arts until their bodies wasted away, the accursed Liche Kings are perhaps the most skilled of undead sorcerers.

Necromancer

Hero (Inf)

Unit Size	Sp	Me	Ra	De	Att	Ne	Pts
1	5	5+	–	4+	1	10/12	85

Special

Individual, Surge (8)

Options

- Heal (3) for +15pts, or free to replace Surge.
- Lightning Bolt (3) for +20pts
- Bane-chant (2) for +15pts
- Mount on an undead horse, increasing Speed to 8 (+15 pts) and changing to Hero (Cav)

Twisted wizards who have dabbled uncautiously with the dark lore of necromancy, these individuals have turned into unliving servants for the lords of the undead.

Mhorgoth the Faceless [1]

Hero (Inf)

Unit Size	Sp	Me	Ra	De	Att	Ne	Pts
1	10	4+	–	6+	1	17/19	270

Special

Bane-chant (4), Fireball (15), Fly, Heal (6), Individual, Lightning Bolt (6), Regeneration (5+), Surge (12), Very Inspiring

Touch of Darkness

If your army includes Mhorgoth, you may upgrade any one non-allied unit in the army (except for Heroes), imbuing it with the arcane power of the Faceless himself (+25 points). The unit thus upgraded has the Regeneration (5+) special rule.

A curse upon the whole world, Mhorgoth the Faceless, the greatest of Necromancers, rises again to continue his unholy quest – turning all living things into undead abominations under his control.

Mhorgoth the Faceless

If Ophidia is the home of necromancy, then it arguably the cause of the greatest threat to stalk Mantica in the present age. Mhorgoth the Faceless is the most powerful Necromancer ever to blight the world.

What little is known of his past is clouded in darkness, and the rest of his story is lost in the mists of time. Regardless of his origins, though, Mhorgoth is hated the length and breadth of the known world, classed as enemy to all living beings. As mad as he is powerful, Mhorgoth has sworn a pact to see every living creature perish, and he will not rest until the world is populated only by the walking dead.

Mhorgoth was once a man, and his talent in the sorcerous arts, even as a child, was far beyond those of any of his kinsmen. It is believed that the Elves took Mhorgoth into their realm when he was but a boy, and schooled him in arcane lore. They did not realise the darkness inside the youth until it was too late.

How and when Mhorgoth was introduced to the dark arts of Necromancy is unknown, but the discovery was met with shock, revulsion and sadness by the Elves. Mhorgoth fled, carrying with him a grimoire containing all his cursed learnings, but he was hunted down and reluctantly sentenced to death.

As his flesh was consumed in the Eternal Flames, Mhorgoth cursed those who had sentenced him, and unleashed the full extent of his dark powers for the first time. When he was spent, there was no living creature within a mile of his location. With his flesh burnt beyond all recognition, Mhorgoth stumbled away in agony. He retreated from the world for many years, during which time his bitterness and madness slowly consumed him.

After two hundred years of self-imposed exile, his life unnaturally prolonged through dark arts, Mhorgoth has at last emerged at the head of the largest Undead legion the world has ever seen. Where he has been, and what wisdom he has acquired, is not yet known, but he is consumed by just one burning aim; to exterminate the living, and repopulate the world with the dead.

MODELLING NOTES

Unit Footprint, Movement Trays and Multibases

If a unit consists of a large number of models, it is far more convenient when moving it around to place a 'movement tray' underneath it – that way you effectively have a single object to move on the battlefield rather than a large number of them (say 20 Elf infantry models). This speeds up gameplay immensely. The ideal movement tray is a piece of plastic, thick cardboard or plasticard that is cut to the exact space occupied by the bases of the models forming the unit, and painted to match the colour of their bases. For example, a regiment of 20 Elf infantry models occupy a rectangluar tray 100mm wide and 80mm deep. If the tray has a little 'lip' around the unit (normally up to a couple of millimetres wide), this does not matter and player should agree to either always ignore the lip when measuring distances (our favourite solution) or to always measure distances from/to it – as long as this is done consistently for all units and both sides, it should not present a problem.

It is even faster, not to mention more practical, to actually glue the models' bases directly onto the tray – that way you have an army that effectively consists of a very small number of individual 'elements' – very compact and easy to store and transport. Some people even go to the next level, and glue their models directly onto the tray, without first placing them on their individual bases. We refer to

these solutions as 'multibases'. Multibases are very useful, but make sure that the multibase itself conforms to the correct size for the ranked up models as if their were mounted onto their individual bases. To continue the example above, you could mount the 20 Elf infantry models directly onto a 100x80mm multibase.

This last way of mounting models directly onto the multibase offers great modelling opportunities, as the multibase can effectively be treated as a mini-diorama in itself, creating great looking and very individual units like the ones shown below. You might even end up with a little more or less than the correct number of models on the multibase – this is fine, but it must be reasonably close to the correct amount, so that there is no chance of misleading your opponents in regards to the real size of the unit. It's best to quickly explain to your opponent what your units are before you play to clarify anything like this.

Unit Leaders, Banners and Musicians

Some units include models that are equipped differently from the rest of the unit – normally the unit's leader, banner-bearer and musician. These models count as being equipped like the rest of the models in the unit and have a purely decorative function in the game – placed in the front rank of your unit, they offer you a good chance of showing off your painting skills and help making the unit look splendid and unique.

An example of a unit on a movement tray.

This unit of elves has been mounted on a single multibase.

This unit's standard bearer model has been placed in the centre of the front rank.